This book would not have been possible without the generous assistance of the following specialists in their field. With deepest gratitude, I thank you all:

Alix Kwan

moxieediting.com.au

Debbie Watson

getitrightproofreading.com.au

Sally-Anne Watson Kane

ontimetyping.com

If you're looking for self publishing assistance, please consider using the services of the above.

Also by Jennifer Mosher:

Business books

Self publishing for Australian authors

Simple Rules for Effective Business Communication

Children's books
(with illustrations by Todd Sharp)

Who Caught the Yawn?

Where Did the Sneeze Go?

(combined in print and separately as ebooks and audiobooks)

Format your book for print with MS Word®

For authors, editors and virtual assistants

For PC users

An IndieMosh
Getting Started
Guide

Jennifer Mosher

This is an IndieMosh book

brought to you by MoshPit Publishing
an imprint of Mosher's Business Support Pty Ltd

PO Box 147
Hazelbrook NSW 2779

indiemosh.com.au

Cataloguing-in-Publication entry is available from the National Library of Australia:
http://catalogue.nla.gov.au/

Title:	Format your book for print with MS Word®
Subtitle:	For authors, editors and virtual assistants
Series:	An IndieMosh *Getting Started* Guide
Author:	Mosher, Jennifer (1961–)
ISBNs:	978-1-925814-90-3 (paperback)

The author has made every effort to ensure that the information in this book was correct at the time of publication. However, the author and publisher accept no liability for any loss, damage or disruption incurred by the reader or any other person arising from any action taken or not taken based on the content of this book. The author recommends seeking third party advice and considering all options prior to making any decision or taking action in regard to the content of this book.

Cover design and layout by Ally Mosher at allymosher.com

Microsoft Word® is a registered trademark of Microsoft Corporation.

Adobe®, InDesign® and Adobe Acrobat® are registered trademarks of Adobe Corporation.

Who is this book for?

- Self publishers

- Editors

- Proofreaders

- Virtual assistants

- Anyone trying to get to grips with MS Word's Styles function

- PC users (or Mac users with strong Mac and Word skills combined)

What do you need?

- A computer

- Microsoft Word or similar with a 'Styles' function, although you will need to 'translate' the instructions to your preferred software

- An understanding of routine computer operating procedures:
  - downloading, moving and renaming files
  - opening, saving and copying files; finding files
  - creating versions of files
  - working with multiple documents open at once
  - copying and pasting within documents and to other documents
  - using the mouse and the cursor to navigate menus.

Contents

1. Introduction 1

2. Let's start with some *Roast Beef, Cheese, Love and Pickles*................**3**

One, two, three, what are we fighting for?....................................4

Why? 4

3. Preparation – the key to success..**5**

Learning aims of this chapter:..5

Create a working copy...5

    Nuke the original text 5

Setting your page size 7

    CreateSpace, KDP and Ingram Spark/Lightning Source page sizes.................7

    Set your page size 7

Setting your margins 9

    Creating left and right hand pages and mirrored margins.............................11

4. Let's start formatting **13**

Learning aims of this chapter:..13

Creating text styles 13

    Getting control of Word's Styles function................................13

    Create a new (main text) style 18

    Apply your main text style 24

    Pick out and format your headings 25

    Modify your Heading 1 Style 29

Decide how your paragraphs are going to look 33

    Block paragraphs or indented? 33

    Test out block paragraphs on your document 34

    Indicating breaks in the narrative within a chapter 35

    Block first paragraph, indented to follow 36

    Left aligned, ragged right edge paragraph variation 37

    Create a *Story First* paragraph style 37

    Apply *Story first* style to the appropriate paragraphs 40

Tidy up unwanted line breaks and delete empty lines 41

    Show paragraph marks and other formatting symbols 41

    Use Find and Replace to locate and remove empty lines 43

    Modify *Story first* style to make the section breaks more identifiable 46

    Tidy up unwanted paragraph indents, tabs and spaces 47

Reinstate italics 47

    Identify italics in the original document 47

    Implement italics in the print document 49

Starting each chapter on a new page 53

    Finding new chapters quickly 53

    Pushing chapter headings down the page 54

Numbering your pages 56

    Opening your footer (and header) 56

    Quickly insert page numbers 56

    Quickly insert a header 58

Use Print Preview to check your formatting work 61

    Reinsert missing footers 62

    Check your insertions using Print Preview 62

5. Title pages and 'front matter' 65

Learning aims of this chapter: 65

The initial pages of your book 65

Setting up *Roast Beef*'s introductory pages 66

Use a Section Break to separate the main body of the book from the front matter 66

Insert an imprint page 67

Fill in some imprint page data 67

Format your imprint data 69

Create a Dedication page 72

Insert a Table of Contents 74

Back to the title page 79

Format your title 79

Format your author name...80

Space your title and author name out...81

Getting the headers and footers right 83

Delete page numbers from initial pages 83

The six Header and Footer options available..85

Page numbering conventions for novels..86

Set Roman numerals for your initial pages...88

6. Let's add some gravy 91

Learning aims of this chapter: 91

Quick summary of where we're at right now..91

Getting an appropriate page size 91

Create a new file for a smaller page size 92

Change the page size 93

Fix things to look good on the new page size 94

Title page 94

Imprint page..95

Body of the story 95

Headers and footers 96

Tweak the margins...96

Vertical Justification 97

Applying vertical justification 97

Fix the last pages of each chapter or section.................................. 97

A note on paragraph spacing for when you're formatting for others............. 98

Widows and Orphans.. 98

Fix widows, orphans and gappy paragraphs by editing the text 100

Fix widows, orphans and gappy paragraphs by tweaking character spacing 102

Tidying up punctuation... 104

Double spacing... 104

Errant spaces at the start of a line.. 105

Ellipsis points... 107

A bit about dashes.. 110

Standardise your dashes... 115

7. Now let's add some spice!...**119**

Learning aims of this chapter: 119

Dynamic Page Headers... 119

Different ToC entries to the page headings 121

Create 'dummy' headings 121

Update the heading text in the document....................................... 123

Update the ToC with the new headings 125

Cleaning up the excess headers in the body of the text........................ 127

Warning 1... 127

Warning 2... 127

8. Time to serve up..**129**

Learning aims of this chapter: 129

Is it cooked?.. 129

Any blank pages?.. 129

Any pages with just a line or two on them? 129

Are page numbers correct? 130

Are headers and footers suppressed where expected? 130

Are blank pages and new sections sitting where expected?...................... 130

Has my ToC updated correctly? 130

Do my 'guff' pages look correct? 131

Do my end pages look correct? 131

Export to PDF 132

Check your PDF 132

Check your PDF's properties 133

Exporting a PDF for print 133

9. Looking back **135**

Why did we have to nuke the original copy of *Roast Beef*? 135

Locating errant formats 136

10. Quick reference **139**

Tools to become *real* friendly with 139

Terms 140

Tailoring 140

Quick Access Toolbar 140

Navigation pane 141

Styles pane 141

Show two pages or more at a time 141

Tricks of the trade 141

11. The wash-up **143**

12. Acknowledgements **145**

13. About the Author **147**

1. Introduction

With the rise in self publishing, many authors are sending their manuscripts directly out to print, either in short runs or as print on demand titles. This freedom and speed to market is fantastic, but the results may not always be quite so wonderful.

In life, we don't know what we don't know, and it's not until someone points out to us that our paragraphs are unevenly spaced, or our headings aren't always the same font size, that we begin to understand that there's more to laying out a book than just typing it and clicking on the formatting tools in the toolbar.

This book has been written to help self-publishing authors, particularly fiction writers, learn the basics of how to format their manuscripts in a more controlled and tidy manner, using the most accessible and affordable tool available to us: Microsoft Word®.

And although this book is aimed at self publishers, it can also be used by editors, proofreaders and virtual assistants to get a handle on book formatting, thus providing them with another potential source of income. Editors and proofreaders in particular may benefit from adding this string to their bows due to their close involvement with the work – they're the people best-qualified to format the book, other than the author, due to their familiarity with its content.

While a lot of the basics are covered in this book, it doesn't get too intricate, so anyone able to follow 'point here, click that' instructions should be able to tidy their manuscript to a reasonably acceptable standard.

The aim is to *get you started* on the road to wrangling your documents the easiest way. (And yes, I realise that it won't seem easy at first, but once you get a handle on it, you'll love it! Well, maybe not *love* …) However, a basic understanding of creating and saving files and operating MS Word (or similar word processing software) is expected. And the sections are written with less and less 'click here, click there' detail to encourage you to remember steps, and to understand what you're looking at on the screen.

I'm an MS-DOS girl from way back, so this book is not aimed at Mac users, and for that I apologise. However, if you're used to using Word on your Mac and translating Microsoft instructions, then you *may* be able to use this book to your benefit. But I have seen first-hand the many differences between the PC and Mac versions of Word 365, and I was quite challenged on more than one occasion!

Throughout the book, references to on-screen choices will be formatted in bold e.g. go to your **Downloads** folder; choose **Insert → Pictures**, etc.

Good luck, and I hope this helps you on your way to painting a prettier word picture!

Jenny Mosher

2. Let's start with some
Roast Beef, Cheese, Love and Pickles

This book walks you through formatting *Roast Beef, Cheese, Love and Pickles*, a short story by Paris Portingale, author of *Art and the Drug Addict's Dog* and *2,000 Jews Walk into a Bar*.

Paris' manuscripts are always very neat and clean, with few errors. However, when you download *Roast Beef* you may notice bits and pieces here and there (or you may not, but you will soon be trained to!), that aren't so neat. These are my adaptions of his manuscript to allow me to show you what to look for and what to do.

Access a copy of *Roast Beef* at **https://jennifermosher.com.au/roastbeef** and use **ParisWrite$** (capitalised as shown) as the password to download the file *RoastBeefbyParisPortingale* at the link labelled *Roast Beef, Cheese, Love and Pickles*.

When you download the file, it may go directly to your **Downloads** folder, depending on how your system is set up, so if you can't find it, check there.

You may wish to create a folder in **My Documents** or elsewhere on your hard drive or flash drive to save the file that you've downloaded so that your *Roast Beef* files (there will be more than one) can be kept together. Perhaps name the folder *Roast Beef* or *Formatting practice*?

Once you've gone through the process of formatting *Roast Beef*, you'll be ready to tackle formatting your own manuscript for print.

One, two, three, what are we fighting for?

The aim is to produce a file where the entire text is controlled by MS Word's Styles function. The sorts of things we will be aiming at are:

1. no empty lines between paragraphs

2. standardised indenting of similar paragraphs

3. standardised headings

4. standardised font usage

5. standardised spacing between different types of paragraph.

Why?

Why is it so important to use Word's Styles functions and not just use ad hoc styling by clicking on formatting icons in the formatting ribbon? So that:

1. we have a 'stable' document which should 'behave' in a predictable manner

2. we have a 'neat' document where every heading is the same size and sits at the same spot on the page, where the page numbers sit in the same place, where the paragraphs are all indented (or not) to the same degree, or to the same degree depending on the type of paragraph. In other words, a document which is acceptable to a reader based on modern standards

3. we can change a font, or a line spacing, or a paragraph indent on a particular *type* of paragraph with just a couple of the clicks of the mouse, without having to go through the entire manuscript searching and clicking one-by-one

4. any changes to headings and/or the page count can be quickly and accurately reflected in the table of contents and/or index (where they exist)

5. you can quickly and easily create a dependable base file for your ebook versions.

3. Preparation – the key to success

Learning aims of this chapter:

- Create a working copy of your book file with 'clean' text

- Create a basic layout for your book

Create a working copy

Rule 1 of Format Club: never use your final draft! That stays 'as is' just in case we make a complete mess of the formatting and have to start again.

So the first thing we're going to do is make a working copy of the file you downloaded, *RoastBeefbyParisPortingale*.

Nuke the original text

I don't know if Mark Coker coined the term 'nuking' for the *Smashwords Style Guide*, or if someone else did, but it is the most apt term for what we're about to do as we start formatting your book for print.

A well-formatted print manuscript can more easily be turned into a dependable ebook file, saving time and effort. And if you save time and effort, you also save ... money! So the first step in our formatting journey is to strip all the formatting from Paris' original manuscript.

Locate the file *RoastBeefbyParisPortingale* (which you downloaded in Chapter 2) and open it in MS Word. Then:

1. Press **Ctrl-A** to highlight all the text in the file.

2. Press **Ctrl-C** to copy all the text in the file.

3. **Open** a new Word document and in the new Word document **right-click** and choose **Paste** or type **Ctrl-V** to paste the final text into the new Word doc. An option should then come up at the very end of the last word of the text so you can choose *how* to paste the text. Right clicking should also bring the options up. Choose the 'A' under **Paste Options** for **Keep Text Only**.

Figure 1 Choose *Keep Text Only* to remove previous formatting

4. Click File → Save as

5. Choose the folder *Roast Beef* or *Formatting Practice* (or whatever you called it) and open that

6. Change the file name to **Roast Beef for Print**

7. Click **Save**.

What you've just done is 'nuke' your first file – stripped it of all its formatting. It is imperative that you do this in the early stages of your formatting career until you get a handle on how to check a document for hidden styling.

You should now have two files in your folder:

- *RoastBeefbyParisPortingale* (the downloaded file, the original, which you won't touch – it's there in case you wish, or need, to start from scratch again), and

- *Roast Beef for Print* (the file you've just created, and which you will work on).

Setting your page size

You may choose almost any page size you like, but of course there will be limitations on printing options and distribution options if you choose anything too out of the mainstream. So when choosing your page size, work backwards – decide how you're going to have your book published, find out the optimal page size for that method, then format your book accordingly.

KDP and Ingram Spark/Lightning Source page sizes

If you're planning to use Amazon's KDP platform or Ingram's Spark or Lightning Source as your print option, or as your main print option, then it's in your best interests to choose one of the Industry Standard sizes.

The most common or popular size these days, is a '6 x 9'. This means the book is trimmed to 6 inches wide by 9 inches high. The publishing industry still speaks in Imperial measurements, but if you're like me and think in metric, this equates to 15.24 cm wide by 22.86 cm high, so use whichever works for the way your version of Word is set up.

Word does have the capacity to convert inches to metric and vice versa, but I've found that it's not always as accurate as you might need when delivering final files. Just a fraction of an inch's difference can cause a file rejection.

Set your page size

Although *Roast Beef* is only a short story, we're going to start with the 6 x 9 format. Later you'll learn how to change the page size.

Now that we've decided to use the 6 x 9 format, ensure that you have the file *Roast Beef for Print* open in Word.

On your (menu) ribbon:

- go to **Layout → Page Setup**

- click on the **arrow** at the bottom right hand corner of the **Page Setup** section to bring up the Page Setup menu.

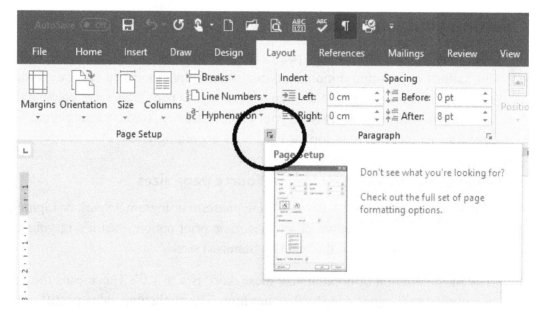

Figure 2: Click on the arrow bottom right to bring up the Page Setup menu

Click on the **Paper** tab, on the **Page Setup** menu. Just below the **Paper Size** option, enter **6** (inches) or 15.24 (cm) in the **Width** field (depending on how your version of Word is set up – whether it's in Imperial or Metric) and then **9** (inches) or **22.86** (cm) in the **Height** field.

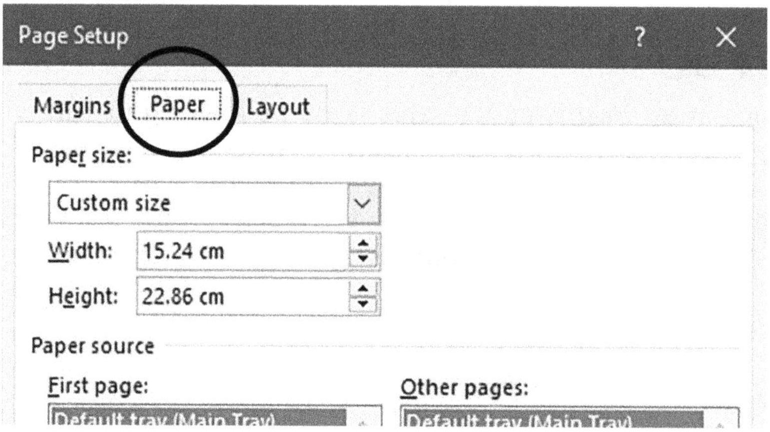

Figure 3: Click on the *Paper* tab to set your page size, then type in the width and height

Towards the bottom of the dialogue box, make sure the words **Whole Document** show in the **Apply to** field. If they don't, then click the drop arrow and choose **Whole Document**.

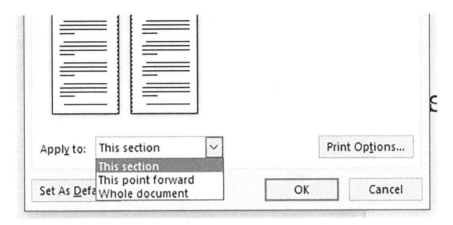

Figure 4: Make sure to choose *Whole document* (not *This point forward* or *This section!*) when setting your page size

Click **OK** and watch *Roast Beef for Print* suddenly resize. Save the file in its new format. Don't worry about what pages are falling where or the size of the margins etc. One step at a time – nothing's in concrete yet!

Setting your margins

Your margins are the spaces around the text. When I format a book, I like to keep between 0.5 and 0.75 inch or between 1.5 and 2 cm spare to the sides of the text so that the reader can hold the book without their thumbs covering the text. There is nothing more annoying than having to change your grip so that you can see the story!

In a 6 x 9 inch book, a 0.75 inch/2 cm margin is no problem, but if you were doing a smaller book, you may want to trim those outside margins to perhaps 1.8 or even 1.5 cm. It doesn't sound like a lot, but it helps. For now, however, we will work with 2 cms.

Starting again with your menu, click on:

- **Layout**

- then click the **drop arrow to the bottom right of Page Setup**

- then click on the **Margins** tab. Change the **Top**, **Bottom**, **Left** and **Right** margin fields to 2 cm or 0.79 inches (depending on how you have Word configured) by typing 2 or 0.79 into each of the four boxes. Again, make sure that towards the bottom of the dialogue box the words **Whole Document** show in the **Apply to** field

- don't click OK yet – turn to the next page!

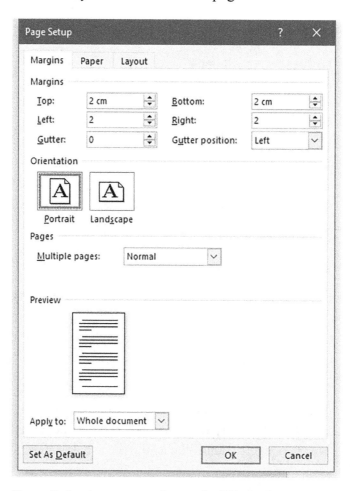

Figure 5: Apply your margins to the *Whole document*

Creating left and right hand pages and mirrored margins

Now, while we're here, we're going to move to the middle of the **Margins** dialogue box, under **Pages**, and in the field for **Multiple pages**, we're going to click the drop-down arrow and change that to **Mirror margins**.

You will notice that the margin options at the top of the dialogue box now say **Top**, **Bottom**, **Inside** and **Outside** (instead of Top, Bottom, **Left** and **Right**).

Click in the field for **Gutter** and change this to 0.5 cm or 0.2 inch. The gutter is an allowance in the middle of the book for that part of the page which will be swallowed up in the binding and it moves the margin out from the centre of the book by that additional amount of space. Click **OK**, then **save the file**.

Figure 6: Set up left and right hand pages by using mirrored margins.

Notes:

4. Let's start formatting

Learning aims of this chapter:

- Working with the Styles pane

- Creating and modifying Styles

- Wrangling the text into consistent paragraph styles

- Understanding the impact of 'nuking' a document

- Creating quick headers and footers

Creating text styles

The beautiful thing about using Microsoft Word to format your book is that you can control all the text with just a few mouse clicks. Obviously, if you have a very complex document with footnotes or endnotes, scientific terms in italics, and/or lots of numbered bullet points and/or numbered chapters, then your formatting life will be a little more complex, but for a novel, it shouldn't take much to lick your manuscript into, well, a book!

You may or may not have used the Styles menu which shows in the menu ribbon across the top of your Word page under the Home tab. Even if you have, you may not understand it all that well, so now you're going to get up close and personal with it, and hopefully understand it a bit better.

Getting control of Word's Styles function

When you 'nuked' the text from your downloaded version of *Roast Beef*, it should have saved in the new document (*Roast Beef for Print*) under your Normal template. If you click anywhere in your Word version of *Roast Beef for Print* and look at the **Styles** menu on the **Home** tab at the top of your page, the button for **Normal** style should be highlighted as active.

Docking the Styles pane

The newer versions of Word allow you to pop the Styles menu out so that you can work with it more easily. If you look at the **Styles** options in the ribbon, at the bottom right hand corner of that part of the ribbon you'll see a small **expansion arrow** pointing downwards at a 45 degree angle. Click on this little arrow and your Styles menu should pop out from the menu ribbon.

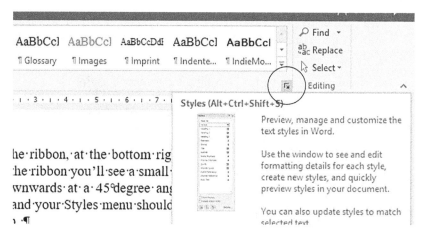

Figure 7: Break your Styles pane out from the menu ribbon by clicking on the menu expansion button at the bottom right hand side of the Styles menu.

If you're lucky, the pane will 'dock' automatically at the left hand side of your screen.

If it's 'floating' on your screen and obscuring your document, point at the top of the Styles pane until you are shown a four-headed arrow, then **left-click drag** it to the left hand side of your screen and dock it there by letting go of your mouse when it's just about in place, to the left of *Roast Beef.*

Dock the Navigation pane

When you're first starting out, and if your screen's big enough, it's worth docking the Navigation pane, too. (See Fig. 8, above.) With the Navigation pane open, you can click quickly between the list of Headings (which represents your table of contents), a summary of the page content, and search results for anything you're searching in the Search field of the Navigation pane.

Having it set on Headings is great when you first start formatting as you can see the document's structure as it begins to take shape.

To dock the Navigation pane as well, click on **Find** at the far right-hand side of your ribbon menu, under the Home tab.

You can resize the width of both the Navigation and Styles panes by hovering your mouse over the dividing line between the two (to resize the Navigation pane) or over the line between the Styles pane and the document until it becomes a two-headed arrow. Then left-click and drag to the left or right to resize the pane in question.

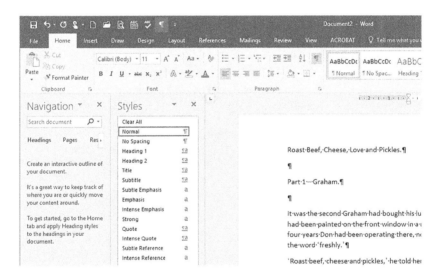

Figure 8: Drag your Styles pane to the left of the screen until it 'docks' next to your document. (You can see here I've docked my Navigation pane, too. You can do this by clicking 'Find' at the far right-hand side of your Home menu.)

In the **Styles pane**, you will see a list of options such as those shown in Fig. 9, over. Yours may be slightly different to those shown in Figure 9, you'll get the general idea.

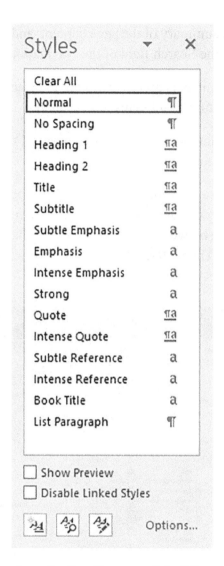

Figure 9: Word will automatically offer you a list of the styles you're most likely to want or need.

Showing only the Styles in the current document

At the foot of the Styles pane, towards the right hand side, you should see **Options...** (refer Fig. 9 above). Click on that to bring up the **Styles Pane Options** dialogue box.

Now, use the drop-down arrows and check boxes to change the options as follows (see Fig. 10 below):

- **Select styles to show:** choose **In current document**
- **Select how list is sorted:** choose **Alphabetical**
- **Select formatting to show as styles:** check all three boxes:
  - **Paragraph level formatting**
  - **Font formatting**
  - **Bullet and numbering formatting**
- **Select how built-in style names are shown:**
  - check **Show next heading when previous level is used**
  - leave *un*checked **Hide built-in name when alternate name exists**
- Ensure that the radio button for **Only in this document** has been chosen and click **OK**.

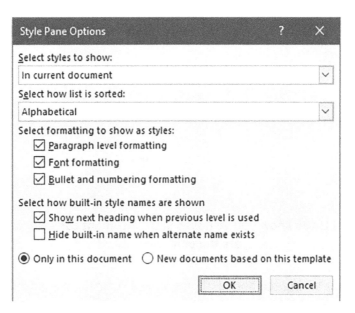

Figure 10: Tell your Styles pane what to show.

After you click OK, the Options dialogue box should close and the only items showing in your Styles pane should be:

- Clear All

- Heading 1

- Normal

Figure 11: You know you've nuked your document correctly when these are the only styles listed!

If you're not seeing the above, then go back over the steps from the start of the chapter and try again, but it's probably something to do with the boxes which need checking in Fig. 10.

Create a new (main text) style

What we're going to do next is create a base style called 'Story' and apply it to the entire document. Following that, we'll select individual items, such as chapter headings, and apply more refined styles to those.

At the bottom of your **Styles pane**, click on the first icon, the one with a star and two As, to bring up the **Create New Style from Formatting** dialogue box.

Figure 12: Click on the first button, bottom left of your Styles pane, to open the Create New Style from Formatting box.

- In the **Name** field type **Story**.

- Ensure that the **Style type** is set to **Paragraph**. Use the drop-down arrow to choose Paragraph if the **Create New Style** box hasn't defaulted to Paragraph.

- Ensure that **Style based on** is set to **Normal**.

- Ensure that **Style** for following paragraph is **Story**.

- Now, to keep it simple for the time being, under **Formatting** choose **Times New Roman** for the font and **12** for the font size. We will play around with different fonts a bit further down the track.

- Make sure that **B**, *I* and U̲ have *not* been selected, and that the next box (font colour) says **Automatic**.

- On the row underneath, click the *fourth* alignment option, for justified text and ensure that single line spacing has been chosen (the *next icon* to the right after the icon for 'justified').

- Moving down below the sample text, make sure that the check box for **Automatically update** is **empty**. (If you've worked with Styles before and found that every time you italicise a word the whole paragraph ends up in italics, it's probably because the Automatically update box had been checked.)

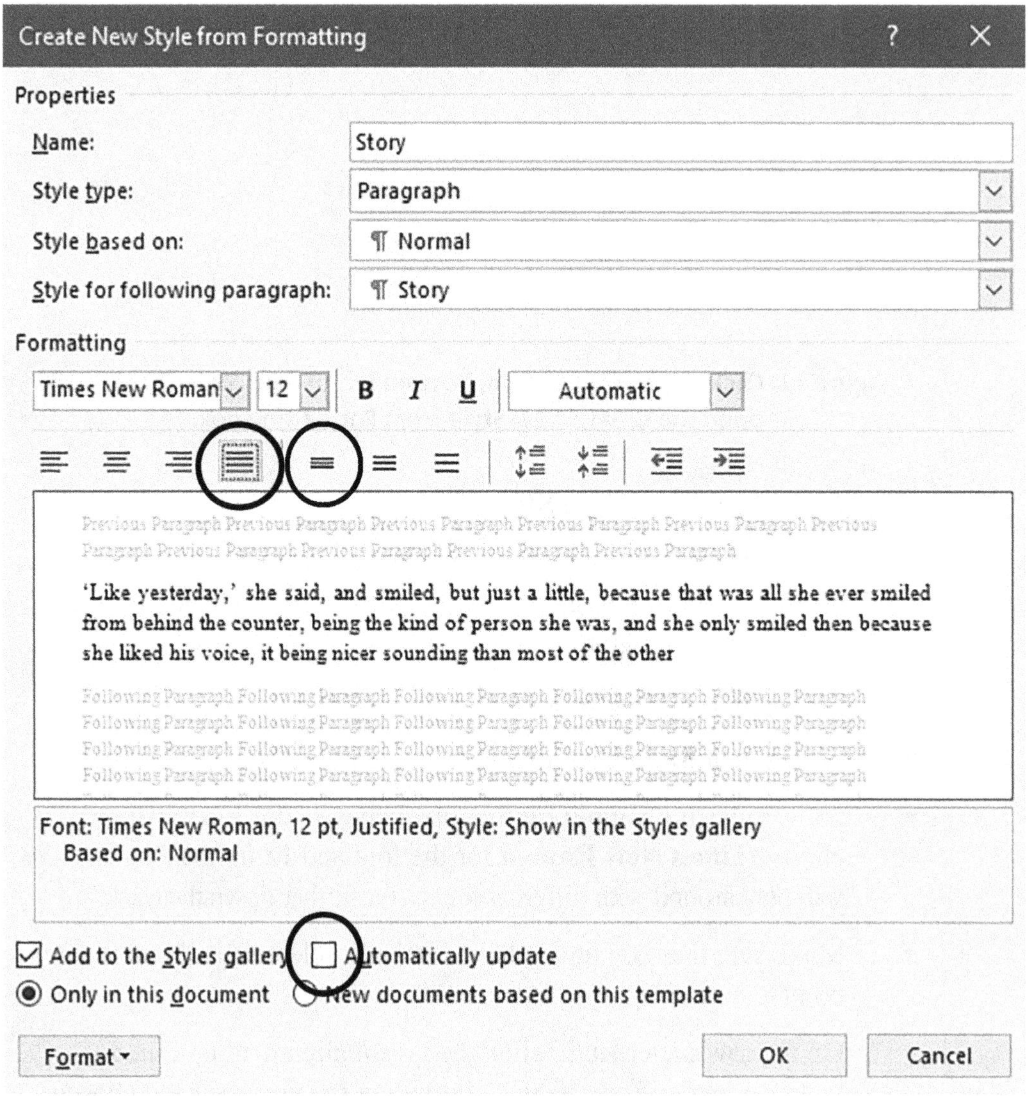

Figure 13: Set up Story style

Next, click on the word **Format** in the bottom left hand corner of the **Create New Style from Formatting** dialogue box:

Font: Times New Roman, No widow/orphan control, Style: Show in the Styles gallery
  Based on: Normal

☑ Add to the Styles gallery   ☐ Automatically update
◉ Only in this document   ○ New documents based on this template

Format ▾   OK   Cancel

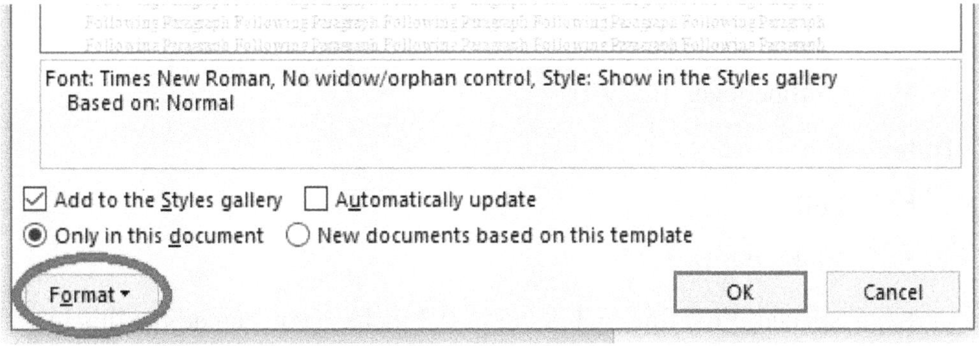

Figure 14 : Additional formatting options are under the Format drop-down menu at the bottom of the Styles formatting dialogue box

Then choose **Paragraph** from near the top of the list.

Figure 15: Select Paragraph... from the Format sub menu

When the **Paragraph** dialogue box opens, make sure that the **Indents and**

Spacing fields are completed as follows (see image on the following page):

General:

- Alignment: Justified
- Outline level: Body Text

Indentation:

- Left: 0
- Right: 0
- Special: First line by 0.8 cm or 0.3 inches (you can adjust this in your own book to your liking)
- Mirror indents: leave *un*checked

Spacing:

- Before: 0 pt (not Auto)
- After: 0 pt (not Auto)
- Line spacing: Multiple 1.2 (you will need to type this in)
- Don't add space between paragraphs of the same style: leave this box *un*checked.

Don't click OK just yet!

Notes:

_____

_____

_____

_____

_____

_____

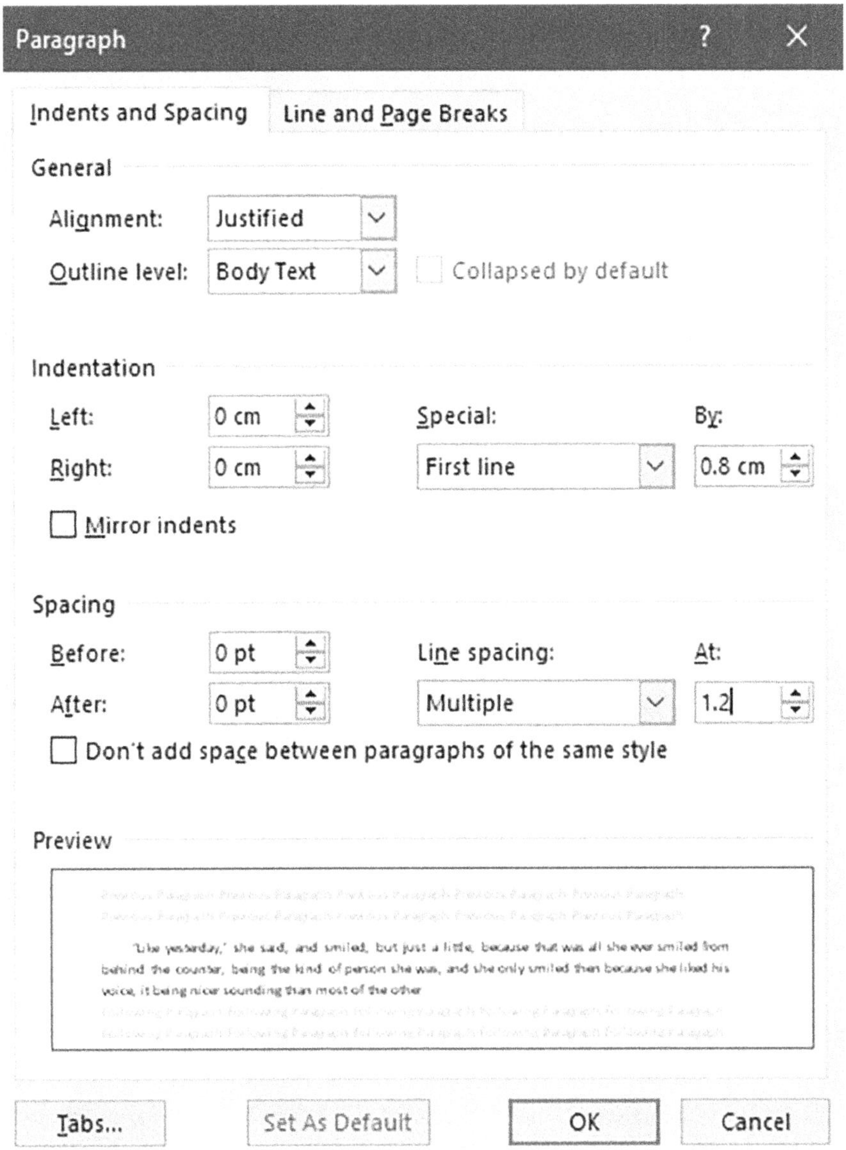

Paragraph   ?   ✕

Indents and Spacing	Line and Page Breaks

General

Alignment: Justified ˅

Outline level: Body Text ˅   ☐ Collapsed by default

Indentation

Left: 0 cm ⬍   Special: By:

Right: 0 cm ⬍   First line ˅   0.8 cm ⬍

☐ Mirror indents

Spacing

Before: 0 pt ⬍   Line spacing: At:

After: 0 pt ⬍   Multiple ˅   1.2|

☐ Don't add space between paragraphs of the same style

Preview

Previous Paragraph Previous Paragraph Previous Paragraph Previous Paragraph Previous Paragraph Previous Paragraph Previous Paragraph Previous Paragraph Previous Paragraph Previous Paragraph

'Like yesterday,' she said, and smiled, but just a little, because that was all she ever smiled from behind the counter, being the kind of person she was, and she only smiled then because she liked his voice, it being nicer sounding than most of the other

Following Paragraph Following Paragraph Following Paragraph Following Paragraph Following Paragraph Following Paragraph Following Paragraph Following Paragraph Following Paragraph Following Paragraph

Tabs...	Set As Default	OK	Cancel

Figure 16: Set up the paragraph specs for Story style

Now click on the **Line and Page Breaks** tab at the top of the **Paragraph** box and make sure that all boxes here are *un*checked. If **Widow/Orphan control** is checked, then uncheck it. We will play with this later.

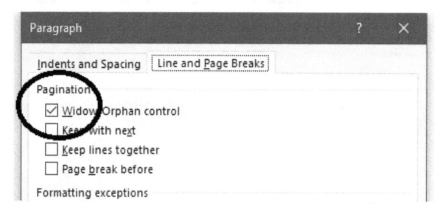

Figure 17: Remove the checkmark from the Widow/Orphan control field

Click **OK** to close the Paragraph formatting box, then click **OK** again to close the Create New Style box. When the Create New Style box closes, have a look at the list of options in your Style menu to the left of your screen. You should now see:

- Clear All
- Heading 1
- Normal
- Story

Apply your main text style

Now that we have a base style for our book, we're going to apply it to all the text. Start by clicking anywhere in *Roast Beef for Print* and then press **CTRL-A** to highlight the entire document. When the whole of the text is highlighted, point at your **Styles pane** and click on **Story**. Watch as your entire document suddenly changes size, justification, line spacing and indentation!

Save your *Roast Beef for Print* file now.

Pick out and format your headings

The next thing we're going to do is find the chapter headings so that they stand out more clearly from the text.

Scroll to the first page of *Roast Beef for Print* and click anywhere in the line which says **Part 1 – Graham**. Don't highlight any particular word – just place your cursor somewhere in that line.

Now point at your **Styles pane** and click on **Heading 1**. Watch as *Part 1 – Graham* suddenly changes from Times New Roman 12 pt into something different! Now we need to rinse and repeat for the rest of the headings in the document.

Notes:

_____

_____

_____

_____

_____

_____

Picking out headings in a longer document

Let's imagine that *Roast Beef* was a hundred pages long. You don't want to be scrolling and looking for each heading if you can help it. If the author has labelled each heading, or at least each main heading, with a repeated word (e.g. Chapter, Book, Part), then you can find these easily and apply the Heading 1 style without the pain of scrolling and looking for the appropriate text.

Start by opening your **Navigation** pane (if you haven't already done so.) Click on **Find** at the far right hand end of your **Home** menu.

The Navigation pane should open and dock to the left or right of your Styles pane. If the Navigation pane is floating, point near the word **Navigation** until your cursor changes into a four-headed arrow, then drag the pane to the left and dock it. Remember – I'd already docked mine:

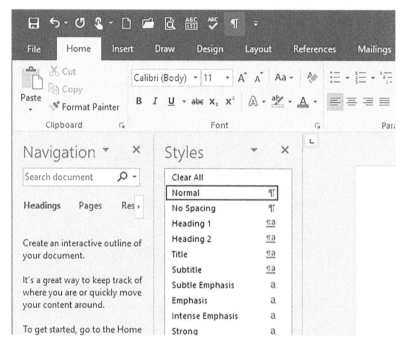

Figure 18: Dock your Navigation pane to the left of your Styles pane

Click in the box showing **Search document** in light grey text, and type the word **part** then click the word **Results** below that. This will bring up a list of instances where the word **part** occurs in the document.

You should get about ten results – some of these will be for words such as 'partly' which are not meant to be headings. Identify the first result where it's clear that it should be formatted as a heading. (Hint: It's **Part 2 – Johanna.**) Click on that result to go to that place in the document. Click *in* that line – anywhere in that line, *without* highlighting any actual word – and then click **Heading 1** in your **Styles** pane. If you don't click *in* that line, Word will only format the word 'part', not the whole line.

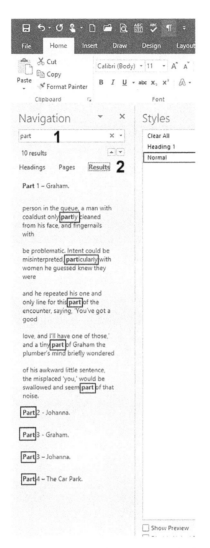

Figure 19: Using the Navigation bar to search the document

Now click the **down arrow** next to the words **Result X of X** below the search box in your **Navigation pane** to be taken to the next instance where 'part' has been used. Use the scroll bar on the Navigation pane if necessary to scroll through the various uses of 'part' or simply click on the next heading visible in the **Results** list. That will take you to that particular use of 'part' in the text. Click *in* that line, then click on **Heading 1** in your **Styles pane**.

Rinse and repeat until you're confident you've picked up all the headings.

If you find that the Navigation pane 'pauses' then click on the down arrow next to the search results to re-activate it.

If you now click the **cross** in the **Navigation search box**, this will remove the word 'part' and clear the search. Then click on **Headings** below the search box and you should see the list of headings now assigned in your document. If you've done well, there should be five 'parts' in numerical order, with two of the headings taking the same number. This is a deliberate mistake which we'll deal with later.

And if you're really alert, you should also notice that you now have a Heading 2 option in your Styles menu. When we clicked on **Options** at the foot of the Styles pane, we made sure to check the box which said **Show next heading when previous level is used**. So each time we apply a new heading level, the next one will appear ready for use. If you apply Heading 2 anywhere in the document, Heading 3 will suddenly become available.

Notes:

_____

_____

_____

_____

_____

_____

_____

_____

_____

_____

_____

Modify your Heading 1 Style

Now, I realise that your inbuilt Heading 1 style is probably about as pretty as mine, so let's do something a little different with it.

It doesn't matter where your cursor is in the document, just *point* (*without* clicking) at the **Heading 1 style** in your **Styles pane**. Pointing at it should bring up a drop arrow on the right hand side.

Click on the **drop arrow** and choose **Modify...** this should open the **Modify Style** box which will look pretty much the same as the **Create Style from Formatting** box.

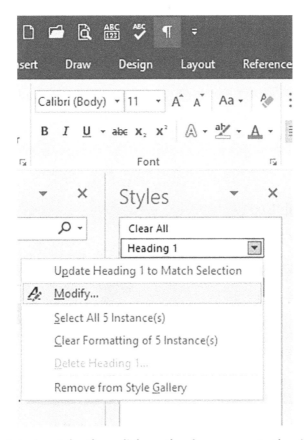

Figure 20: Point at a style, then click on the drop arrow to the right of the style name to access tools to modify it.

Let's choose **Berlin Sans FB** in a size **16** font, and make sure that **Automatic** has been chosen for the colour (same row, to the right of your font options).

In the next row, let's choose **Centre** alignment, **single line spacing** (as we did before).

Make sure that **Automatically update** has *not* been checked, then click on **Format** in the lower left hand side and choose **Paragraph** from near the top of the pop-up menu to bring up the Paragraph dialogue box. (Click on the **Indents and Spacing** tab at the top of the Paragraph dialogue box if the **Line and Page Breaks** tab is sitting in front.)

Complete the paragraph formatting fields as follows:

General:

- Alignment: Centred
- Outline level: Level 1 (this may be greyed out and inaccessible)

Indentation:

- Left: 0
- Right: 0
- Special: None
- Mirror indents: leave *un*checked

Spacing:

- Before: 24 pt
- After: 12 pt
- Line spacing: Single (leave the **At** field blank)
- Don't add space between paragraphs of the same style: leave *un*checked.

Click **OK** to close the Paragraph formatting box, then click **OK** again to close the **Modify Style** box.

Watch as your headings all jump into their own space in the middle of the line!

After the **Modify Style** box closes, have another look at the list of options in your Styles pane to the left of your screen. You should now see:

- Clear All
- Heading 1
- Heading 2
- Normal
- Story

Again, notice how, now that we've used Heading 1, the menu has brought in Heading 2 for us, ready for when we need it. If we use Heading 2, then it will bring in the Heading 3 option. This is because we checked **Show next heading** when previous level is used when we set our Style options after clicking **Options...** at the foot of the Styles pane.

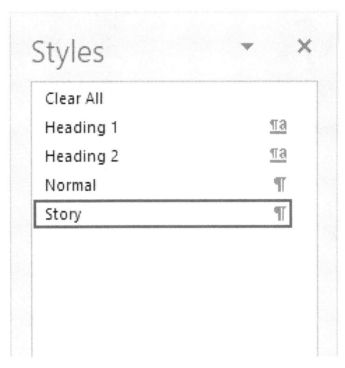

Figure 21: Word has automatically added Heading 2 to the Styles pane

If you can't recall that step, then click on **Options...** again to bring up your **Style Pane Options**, and you should see the box that you checked saying **Show next heading when previous level is used**.

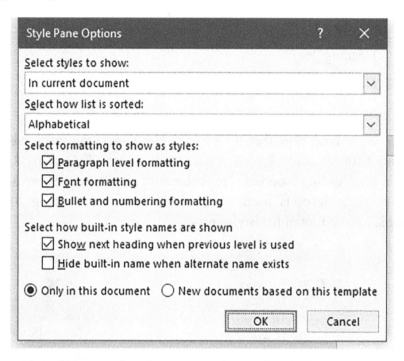

Figure 22: Making sure that the next Heading style will show up after we use a previous level.

Notes:

Decide how your paragraphs are going to look

Generally speaking, you will want all your paragraphs to be 'justified' – like this paragraph – so that the text stretches out across the page making an even line down the left and right hand sides of the page. The letters are spaced as evenly as possible, as are the spaces between the words so that there are no gaps at the right hand edge of each line.

Block paragraphs or indented?

At the moment, there is no additional spacing between our paragraphs as they are each indented on the first line. If you look at any page of *Roast Beef for Print*, the paragraphs should be fairly evenly spaced on the page, except where, perhaps, there is an additional blank line between paragraphs. (Again, these have been deliberately introduced to help with these exercises.)

There are two main paragraph formatting styles when publishing a printed book, and now it's time to decide which one you'd like to use. Your options are:

1. Block paragraphs (not indented) with a small space after each paragraph to help the reader see where the next paragraph starts (similar to this book), are usually used in non-fiction books.

2. Indented paragraphs, with no space between them, where the first paragraph in every section (i.e. chapter or subsection within a chapter) will be a block paragraph (not indented), are usually used in fiction books, such as novels. So this would be the first paragraph of the chapter or sub section. (It's justified across the line and there is no automatic gap after the last line.)

    This would be the second paragraph. It's justified across the line, too, but indented. And subsequent paragraphs would look like this one.

    This would be the third paragraph. And again, subsequent paragraphs would look like this and the one above.

    And this would be the fourth paragraph and again, all paragraphs would look like this until the end of the chapter or section.

Test out block paragraphs on your document

First up, click anywhere in the ordinary text of your document, so that you don't accidentally reformat a heading!

The easiest thing to start with is testing out block paragraphs. Point at your **Story** style in the **Styles pane** to the left of your screen until you see the drop arrow come up on the right hand side. Click the drop arrow, then click **Modify** to open the **Modify Style** dialogue box.

Now click on **Format** in the lower left hand side and choose **Paragraph** from near the top of the pop-up menu and change the **Indentation** for **Special** from **First line by** 0.8 cm or 0.3 inches, to **(none)**.

Then change the **Spacing After** to **6 pt**.

All other specs will remain as you created them previously:

General:

- Alignment: Justified
- Outline level: Body Text

Indentation:

- Left: 0
- Right: 0
- Special: **None**
- Mirror indents: *un*checked

Spacing:

- Before: 0 pt (not Auto)
- After: **6 pt**
- Line spacing: Multiple 1.2
- Don't add space between paragraphs of the same style: *un*checked.

Click **OK** to close the Paragraph formatting box, then click **OK** again to close the **Modify Style** box.

Watch as your paragraphs all align to the left of the page and small but noticeable gaps are created between each one.

Indicating breaks in the narrative within a chapter

If you scroll through your copy of *Roast Beef for Print* now, you should see larger gaps every now and again where Paris has inserted a blank line or two to indicate a break in the narrative within a chapter. Quite often, he has done this to indicate the next day within that part of the story.

In-chapter section breaks within a story can be indicated in several ways. With the block paragraphs that we have now, my suggestion would be to put some sort of indicator in the blank lines as this helps avoid having unusual spacing when you get to the end or beginning of the next page. I generally recommend some centred symbols, along the lines of the following:

However, rather than going down this path, we're going to do something different with this manuscript.

Notes:

_____

_____

_____

_____

_____

Block first paragraph, indented to follow

If you look at many modern novels, you will notice that the first paragraph in each chapter (and in each section/sub-section within a chapter) is a block paragraph i.e. it is fully justified across the line and it's *not* indented. Subsequent paragraphs are indented and there is no additional space between the paragraphs. That's what we're going to do with *Roast Beef for Print*.

First we need to set our **Story style** back to being indented with no space between the paragraphs, as this will cover the bulk of the paragraph formatting. Point at the right hand end of the **Story** style in your **Styles pane**, click on the drop arrow and choose **Modify**. This should open the **Modify Style** dialogue box.

Now click on **Format** in the lower left hand side and choose **Paragraph** from near the top of the pop-up menu and change the **Indentation** for **Special** from **(none)** to **First line** by 0.8 cm or 0.3 inches, and the Spacing After to **0 pt**. Keep the other specs you created previously.

General:

- Alignment: Justified
- Outline level: Body Text

Indentation:

- Left: 0
- Right: 0
- Special: First line by 0.8 cm or 0.3 inches
- Mirror indents: leave *un*checked

Spacing:

- Before: 0 pt (not Auto)
- After: 0 pt (not Auto)
- Line spacing: Multiple 1.2 (you will need to type this in)
- Don't add space between paragraphs of the same style: *un*checked.

Click **OK** to close the Paragraph formatting box, then click **OK** again to close the **Modify Style** box. Watch as your paragraphs all indent again and the gaps between paragraphs are closed up.

Left aligned, ragged right edge paragraph variation

You may notice special paragraphs within a book which aren't justified but are perhaps merely left aligned. These are sometimes called 'ragged right edge'. This paragraph is an example of a left aligned, or ragged right edge, paragraph. You can see how it all lines up on the left but the letters are given only the space they need and so the line bears only the number of words which will fit, leaving gaps at the end of each line at the right hand side.

For this exercise we'll assume that everything in *Roast Beef for Print* will be fully justified, not left aligned or ragged right edge.

Create a *Story First* paragraph style

The next thing to do is scroll to the beginning of *Roast Beef for Print* and click anywhere in the very first paragraph, the one beginning with *It was the second time*.

If you look at your **Styles pane** to the left, you will see that **Story style** has been highlighted, indicating that this is the format which has been applied to this paragraph.

As this is the first paragraph in the chapter, we want it to be a block, fully left-aligned paragraph, and we want it to be spaced a bit after the preceding text or heading, so we're going to create a new style to do that for us.

At the bottom of your **Styles pane**, click on the first icon, the one with a star and two As, to bring up the **Create New Style from Formatting** dialogue box. In the **Name** field type **Story first**.

Ensure that the **Style type** is set to **Paragraph**. Use the drop-down arrow to choose **Paragraph** if the **Create New Style** box hasn't defaulted to Paragraph.

Ensure that **Style based on** is set to **Story**. This means that if you change the format for **Story** style, this new style will change with it. For instance, you or your author may decide that you wish to change the font used in the book. By having **Story first** based on **Story**, you only need to change the font for the **Story** style and it will also change the font for **Story first**.

Ensure that **Style for following paragraph** is **Story**.

Now, to keep it simple for the time being, ensure that under **Formatting** it reflects **Times New Roman** for the font and **12** for the font size. Make sure that **B**, *I* and <u>U</u> have *not* been selected, and that the next box (font colour) says **Automatic**. On the row underneath, ensure that the fourth alignment option, for **justified text** has been chosen. Moving down underneath the sample text, make sure that the check box for **Automatically update** is empty.

Next, click on the word **Format** in the bottom left hand corner and choose **Paragraph** from near the top of the list. When the **Paragraph** dialogue box opens, make sure that the **Indents and Spacing** fields are completed as follows (you should only have to change the **Indentation – Special** option to **(none)**):

General:

- Alignment: Justified
- Outline level: Body Text

Indentation:

- Left: 0
- Right: 0
- Special: **(none)** (leave the **By** field blank)
- Mirror indents: leave *un*checked

Spacing:

- Before: 0 pt (not Auto) (Later on we will change this, but for now it needs to be zero.)
- After: 0 pt (not Auto)
- Line spacing: Multiple 1.2
- Don't add space between paragraphs of the same style: *un*checked.

Now click on the **Line and Page Breaks** tab at the top of the **Paragraph** box and make sure that all boxes here are *un*checked. If **Widow/Orphan control** is checked, then *un*check it. Click **OK** to close the Paragraph formatting box, then click **OK** again to close the Create New Style box.

When the **Create New Style** box closes, have a look at the list of options in your **Styles pane** to the left of your screen. You should now see:

- Clear All

- Heading 1

- Heading 2

- Normal

- Story

- Story first

And you should also see that your first paragraph is now a block paragraph.

Save your file.

Notes:

_____

_____

_____

_____

_____

_____

_____

Apply *Story first* style to the appropriate paragraphs

Now let's scroll through *Roast Beef for Print* and apply the **Story first** style where appropriate. Story first should be applied to the first paragraph in each chapter, and the first paragraph in any sub-section within a chapter – where the narrative 'breaks' slightly from its previous topic.

You've applied it to the first paragraph in the document, so the next paragraph where it should apply is the one beginning *The next day was a Wednesday and at 12.30 Graham ...* on page 2. (You can see that Paris has left extra space between this paragraph and the one prior to indicate a change in the narrative within that chapter.) **Click** anywhere you like in that paragraph, but *don't* highlight any particular word – just place your cursor somewhere in that paragraph. Now click on the **Story first** style in the **Styles pane** and watch as that paragraph left aligns.

Continue scrolling through and applying **Story first** in this manner to the first paragraph in each chapter or section within a chapter. Generally speaking, other than the first paragraph in every chapter, the applicable paragraphs *within* a chapter will each be after an empty line.

At this stage, do not remove the empty lines between paragraphs.

When finished, save your file.

Notes:

Tidy up unwanted line breaks and delete empty lines

Many authors add empty lines to their documents. Some do it because they want space between each section, some want space between each paragraph and don't know how to achieve it, while others do it in some places and not others. Some authors use the Enter key repeatedly to start a new chapter on a new page, rather than using a page break. Whatever the reason, it's best to remove empty lines wherever possible, otherwise you'll risk having them turn up at the top of a page and other annoying places!

Now that we've applied the block and indent formats to *Roast Beef*, we need to remove the empty paragraphs/empty lines between paragraphs. If you have your paragraph marks turned on, you'll also notice empty paragraphs between the chapter headings and the first paragraph of each chapter. We will be working soon to remove these. But first …

Show paragraph marks and other formatting symbols

Formatting symbols help you see why your document is behaving the way it is. They show you where the space bar has been pressed, where the enter key has been pressed, where tabs have been inserted – all sorts of wonderful behind-the-scenes things that can make your document look less pretty than it should!

SPOILER ALERT – THIS IS GOING TO MAKE YOUR DOCUMENT LOOK UG-LEEEE!

The sample below shows:

- every instance of **Enter** (¶)
- every instance of a **soft return** (↵) (where **Enter** and **Shift** were pressed at the same time)
- every single **space** (·)
- every non-breaking space (°)
- every **Tab** (→):

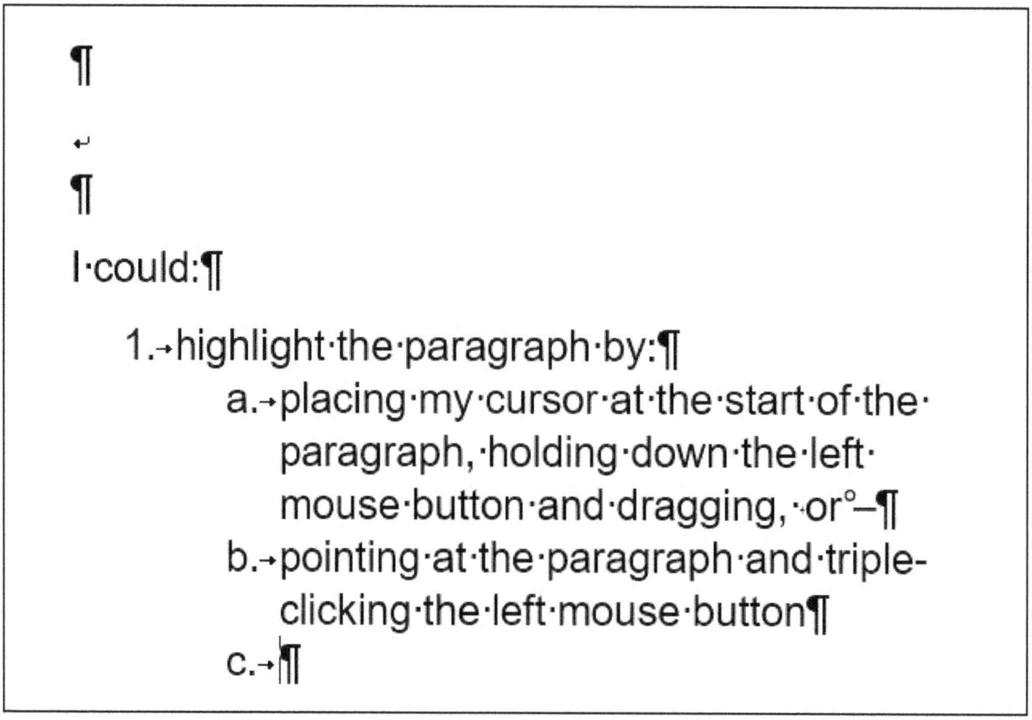

¶

↵

¶

I·could:¶

   1.→highlight·the·paragraph·by:¶
         a.→placing·my·cursor·at·the·start·of·the·
         paragraph,·holding·down·the·left·
         mouse·button·and·dragging,··or°–¶
         b.→pointing·at·the·paragraph·and·triple-
         clicking·the·left·mouse·button¶
         c.→¶¶

Figure 23: What paragraph marks and other formatting symbols look like when you reveal them. Ugly, yes, but ever so useful!

Use Find and Replace to locate and remove empty lines

While *Roast Beef for Print* is a small document and you could easily scroll through and identify spurious line breaks, we're going to pretend that it's a full-size novel and practise what we'd do under those circumstances.

Go to page 1 of *Roast Beef* and place your cursor somewhere in the title at the very top of that page.

Open your **Find and Replace** menu by clicking on the drop arrow at the end of the **Search document** field in your **Navigation pane** and choosing **Replace**.

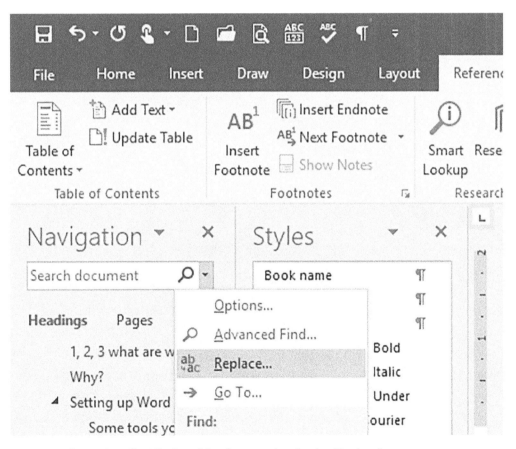

Figure 24: The Find and Replace option in the Navigation pane.

Click in the first field, the **Find what** field, **delete any pre-existing search terms**, then click on **More > >** at the bottom left of the dialogue box. When the dialogue box expands down (or up, depending on where the Find and Replace menu opens on your screen), click on the drop arrow next to **Special** at the bottom of the dialogue box to bring up the list of, well, special options!:

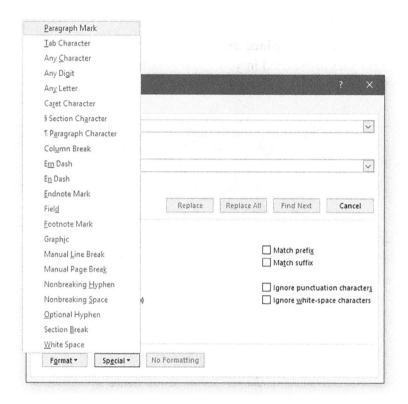

Figure 25: Telling Word to search for a paragraph mark.

Choose **Paragraph Mark** from the list by left clicking. This should place **^p** in the **Find what** field. Go to the **Find what** field and either copy and paste the **^p** next to the existing **^p** in the **Find what** field again, or else type it, so that your **Find what** field has **^p^p** in it. This is telling Word that you want to search for two paragraph breaks in a row.

In the **Replace with** field, either type, or copy and paste, **^p**.

We are now telling Word to remove all instances of two paragraph breaks in a row and replace with just one.

Click on **< < Less** under the **Replace with** field label to hide the bottom part of the dialogue box so that you can see more of your screen. Then click on **Find next** to be taken to the first pair of consecutive paragraph marks. Click **Replace** to replace the two paragraph marks with one, thus removing the empty or blank line.

Word will now highlight the next pair of consecutive empty paragraph marks. Click **Replace** to change them to one, to remove the empty or blank line, and repeat until Word tells you there are no more in the document.

If you're really game, you can click **Replace All** and Word will zoom through the document and do all the changes for you in one hit, but when you're first using Find and Replace, it's a good idea to make changes one at a time until you get a feel for the sorts of things you may not have realised will get fixed.

When Word tells you that it's found them all, run the Find and Replace one more time, just in case. If there were three paragraph breaks in a row, then you won't have solved the problem completely!

When finished, close your Find and Replace dialogue box.

Notes:

Modify *Story first* style to make the section breaks more identifiable

Now that we've removed the empty lines, it's hard to tell where each sub section within each chapter starts. Sure, we have a block paragraph, but only someone who understands what you were trying to achieve with your formatting will notice those block paragraphs, and many people noticing them will think they're a formatting error – that someone forgot to indent them! So we need to make them more obvious.

The easiest way to do this is to format them so that there is a leading space beforehand, pushing them down and away from the prior paragraph. This is quickly and easily achieved by modifying our Story first style.

Point at the **Story first** style (being careful *not* to choose the base Story style!) in your **Styles pane** and click the drop arrow at the right hand side. Choose **Modify** to open the **Modify Style** dialogue box. Click on **Format** at the bottom left hand side of the dialogue box, and then on **Paragraph** in the context menu. When the **Paragraph** dialogue box opens, on the **Indents and Spacing** tab, change the **Before 0 pt** to **Before 18 pt**, to insert a noticeable space *before* each **Story first** paragraph. Click **OK** to close the Paragraph dialogue box and then **OK** again to close the Modify Style dialogue box, and then scroll through *Roast Beef for Print* to ensure that each paragraph marking the start of a new section has some noticeable space before it.

Notes:

_____

_____

_____

_____

_____

_____

_____

_____

Tidy up unwanted paragraph indents, tabs and spaces

Now that you've cleaned up the ad hoc spacing between paragraphs and standardised the spacing and justification of them all, you'll be able to identify any remaining spurious keystrokes that have made their way into your document.

Scroll through your document making sure that your paragraph marks and other formatting symbols are showing, and keep an eye out for:

- tab marks indenting a paragraph

- blank spaces at the beginning of a line or paragraph

- any other sentence or line which has a tab or unwanted space within it.

Delete each item as you go and watch the text tidy itself up.

Reinstate italics

Not all books will have italics in them, but so that you can see an easy way to reinstate them, I've added a couple of instances of italics to the original *Roast Beef* and we'll work through getting those into the print file now.

Identify italics in the original document

The first thing we need to do is identify the italics in the source document. Open the original *RoastBeefbyParisPortingale* file (if it's not already open). If you're presented with the option to **Enable Editing**, then click on that. Click **Find** (far right on your Home menu) to open your **Navigation** pane. Open your **Find and Replace** dialogue box. Clear any data from both the **Find what** and **Replace with** fields, then put your cursor in the **Find what** field. Click **More → Format**. In the Format box, choose **Font** then click on **Italic** under **Font style** then **OK**.

Now place your cursor in the **Replace with** box, click **Format → Font → Italic** and choose **Red** for your **Font colour**. Click **OK**, then **Less**, then **Find Next**. (If red is hard for you to see, then choose a different colour – something which is going to stand out for you against the black.)

If you find that you're getting a 'not found' result, check to make sure that there is absolutely *no* text in either the **Replace** or **Find** fields, not even an empty space from the Space bar. This field needs to be completely blank, otherwise Word will be looking for whatever text is in there, but in italics. And that ain't gonna help you at all!

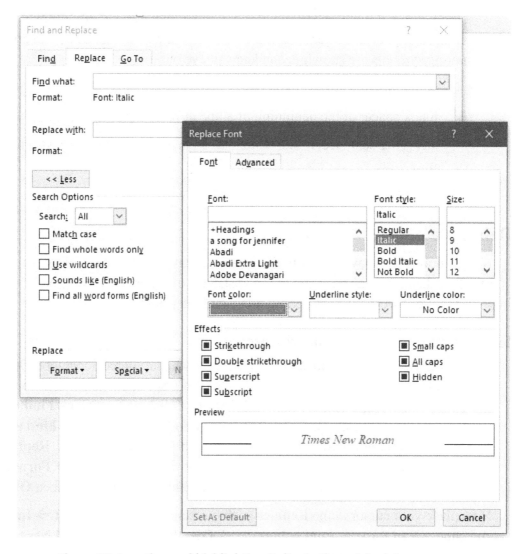

Figure 26: Locating and highlighting italics in the original document

When you are taken to the first use of italics in the original document, click **Replace**. This will change that section of the text to red (or whatever colour you chose) then it will immediately place your cursor at the next instance of italics. Click **Replace All** to replace all italics in the original document with red italics without inspecting each individually.

When you've finished, click in the **Find** box, then click **More** >> then **No Formatting** at the bottom of your **Find and Replace** box, then repeat with your cursor placed in the **Replace** box, to clear all italics and red italics instructions. If you don't do this, you will tear your hair out wondering why the Search function isn't finding things that you know are there! (I have learnt this one from hard, hair-pulling experience.)

Close your Find and Replace box.

Save the original document with the red italics. Although this is the original, it won't take much to turn the italics back to black, should that be required.

Notes:

_____

_____

_____

_____

_____

_____

_____

_____

_____

_____

Implement italics in the print document

Now ensure you have both documents open on your screen – the original and the one that you're formatting for print. If not, then open whichever one is still closed.

Size your two documents so that they can sit side-by-side on your screen. If you're using Windows 8 or higher, you should be able to drag one document to your left or right until it 'snaps' to half-size, then be able to choose the other document to fill up the other half of the screen. I tend to work with the original document to the left and the new file to the right.

Move to the very start of both documents and click at the top of each. Then go to the original *Roast Beef* and start scrolling down until you see some red italics. The first instance you find should be the word **Sorry**.

In *Roast Beef for Print*, click in the **Search field** at the top of the **Navigation pane** and type in the word **sorry**. Don't worry about using a capital 's'. Click **Results** so that you can see how often it appears in the story. Look for the use of **Sorry** which matches the italicised version in *Roast Beef* – compare the surrounding text in both documents to identify the right **Sorry**.

Figure 27: Finding the correct instance of 'Sorry' to italicise

When you've done found the right one, click on the **Result** you want to be taken to in *Roast Beef for Print*.

Double-click on the Sorry which needs to be italicised (to highlight the entire word), and on the (pop-up) context menu which appears, click the *I* to format Sorry in italics. Make sure you don't italicise the question mark or the quote marks on either side of the word. Alternatively, click Ctrl-I or the *I* on the Home menu.

Save your document.

Go back to *RoastBeefbyParisPortingale* and scroll to the next instance of red italics. In *Roast Beef for Print*, put that word or phrase (you can copy and paste from *RoastBeefbyParisPortingale*) in the **Search field** in the **Navigation pane** in *Roast Beef for Print*, click **Results** and find the correct place in the document which needs to be italicised. Double-click on the word or phrase to highlight it, then italicise.

Rinse and repeat until you're sure you've managed to identify and reinstate all instances of italics.

Save your *Roast Beef for Print* document and close *RoastBeefbyParisPortingale*. You can save the changes to *RoastBeefbyParisPortingale* if you wish.

Yes, Virginia, reinstating italics is a pain

You're probably thinking, 'What a pain!', and you'd be right: reinstating italics *is* a pain, particularly if you're working on a non-fiction book. It's one of those unfortunate things which needs to be done, but if you approach it the right way it needn't be too bad.

If I have a lot of italics to reinstate, I find some quiet background music and a nice hot cuppa or some chilled water helps keep me fresh. Don't drink alcohol – you'll be falling asleep at your desk in no time! Just approach the task with a zen attitude, allow yourself the time to do it properly, and that will help take the stress out of it.

If the text you're working on has whole paragraphs in italics, for instance, where characters are 'thinking' to each other instead of speaking out loud, you can create a style called 'Story think', for example, which is based on Story, but which applies italics to the entire paragraph. Then apply 'Story think' to each of those paragraphs to save time. It won't help for individual words or phrases in larger paragraphs, but will save *some* clicking.

If the text you're working on refers to the same italicised words more than once e.g. a song title, then use the Navigation search bar to find every instance to help reduce the amount of scrolling you have to do! Or, use **Find and Replace** and choose **Replace All** to replace all at once. This works really well for things such as song title, book titles, ship names etc where every instance will be in italics.

However, be careful! If you have a ship named, say, the *SS Jennifer* and you know that you've used both *SS Jennifer* and 'the *Jennifer*' throughout the manuscript, you'll have to Find and Replace for both versions.

And then if by chance you also have a character called 'Jennifer' (because you're totally devoted to me and can think of no other name for your boats or your characters, and for that I thank you), you'll have to be careful how you approach replacing 'Jennifer' where it *doesn't* have the 'SS' in front!

Notes:

_____

_____

_____

_____

_____

_____

_____

_____

_____

_____

_____

_____

Starting each chapter on a new page

With most books, it's nice to start a new chapter on a new page. It helps the reader feel that they're getting somewhere and lets the book 'breathe' a little. Occasionally this isn't practical – some books are so long that you need to run the chapters continuously, breaking pages only for larger sections of the story – but for *Roast Beef* it's good practice to see some of your options.

To start a chapter on a new page, you need to insert a **Page Break**. There are four ways to do this:

1. You can click in front of the chapter name/heading, go to **Layout** on your ribbon, click on **Breaks** and choose **Page** from the top of the menu.

2. Or, you can go to **Insert** on your ribbon and click on **Page Break** at the left hand side of the ribbon.

3. Or, you can click in front of each chapter heading, then press **Ctrl-Enter** to create a page break. This is often the quickest option.

4. You can format your chapter level headings to always have a page break beforehand. Click on the style for the chapter headings to **Modify style**, choose **Format → Paragraph** and click on the **Line and Page Breaks** tab and check the **Page Break Before** box.

For various reasons I don't recommend the last option. It works if you know what you want, but I find it also prevents me using some other controls that I sometimes like or need to apply.

Finding new chapters quickly

You have two ways of finding your new chapter headings. The slow way is to scroll manually through the document clicking in front of each as you find them. This is okay, but can lead to you missing one (or more, in a larger document!).

The easy way is to click on **Headings** below the Search box in the **Navigation pane** to display all the chapter headings in a list down the side of your page. You can then just click on each heading in the Navigation pane list to go to that one, then click in the document at the start of each heading and insert a page break.

You should have five chapters showing in your list (Part 1, Part 2, two labelled Part 3 and one Part 4), and if you insert a page break prior to each one, you will end up with *Roast Beef, Cheese, Love and Pickles* on the first page by itself, and then each chapter will start at the top of a new page.

Pushing chapter headings down the page

One of the weird things Word does is that it ignores inbuilt or leading space before text in a Heading style when that format appears on the first line of a page after a 'normal' page break.

When we created our Heading 1 style for our chapter headings, we formatted it to **Before 24 pt**. And yet, when you look at your headings, they're all sitting flush at the top of the page! (There is a way around this, by formatting the style to always have a page break beforehand, but if you do that, then you can't use the heading in the middle of a page and if you need to do that on a rare occasion, it will drive you crazy trying to remember why you keep getting a page break!)

Personally, I like a little space at the top of a new chapter, and the quickest way to achieve this is to insert a blank line prior to each heading, so that the heading style can 'activate' the 'space before' instruction.

In a small document such as this, it's easy to just click on each chapter heading in the **Navigation pane**, and then hit **Enter** after placing the cursor in front of each heading. However, in a larger document this could take you a little while, so let's use Word's automation to help.

The other problem is that each new blank line will be formatted as Heading 1 and we don't want that – we want it to have Story style.

Open the **Replace** box again (**Navigation pane → Drop arrow at end of Search box → Replace…**), click on **More > >** then **Special** and choose **Manual Page Break** from the list for the **Find** field.

In the **Replace with** field repeat **Manual Page Break** (or copy and paste from the Find field) and then click **Special** again and choose **Paragraph Mark**.

Alternatively, type **^m** in the **Find field** and **^m^p** in the **Replace with** field.

Click **< < Less** to collapse your **Find and Replace** dialogue box then **Find Next** to find the first page break. Click **Replace**, then repeat as you find each page break.

This process searches for every deliberate page break (i.e. not the ones that occur naturally as your text flows from page to page but the ones you inserted), and will insert a blank line *after* every page break – placing it at the top of the next page, immediately before the heading on that page.

When you've finished, you will see that your headings have each been pushed down a bit (by the empty line plus the leading space included in Heading 1), giving them a little more room to 'breathe' and thus indicating the chapter beginnings a little more obviously.

Notes:

Numbering your pages

To help your readers find their way around the book, it's always a good idea to number the pages. This can be done in a couple of ways, but for now we're going to keep it relatively simple and just place a number at the bottom of each page, in the centre of the page.

Before you start, take a note of the page count of your document.

Opening your footer (and header)

The repeated headings at the top of every page – the ones that tell you what book you're reading, or what chapter you're in, or who the author is – are called headers. The details at the bottom of every page are called footers.

When you open a header or a footer in Word, you have access to both at the same time, but not to the main part of the document. When you're working in the main part of the document, you can't accidently type over a header or footer. However, when you're working in the main part of the document, you should still be able to *see* the headers and footers, and vice versa.

To open your headers and footers is easy. Point at the space at the very bottom or very top of any page and double-click with your mouse. If you point and click correctly, your document should then show the **Header** and **Footer** spaces, and the **Header and Footer Tools** menu should be active on your ribbon.

The alternative is to go to **Insert** on your ribbon, and just past the halfway mark from the left you can click on **Header**, **Footer** or **Page Number** – depending on which one you're wishing to open or insert.

Quickly insert page numbers

To get started quickly with our page numbering, we're going to take the last option from the above list. Go to **Insert** on your ribbon, and to the right of **Comment**, you'll see the options for **Header**, **Footer** and **Page Number**. Click on the drop arrow to the right of **Page Number** and choose **Bottom of Page** and then from the list choose **Plain Number 2**. This will place a simple page number in the centre of each page at the bottom.

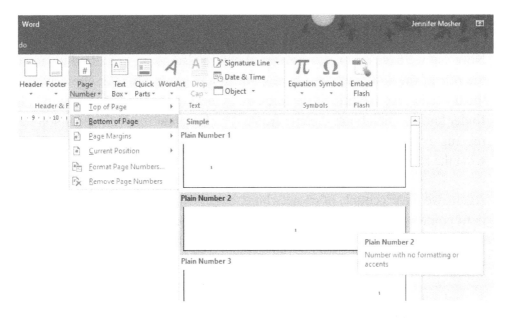

Figure 28: Inserting an automatic page number at the bottom of each page

Spacing your page numbering a little more agreeably

Now, you'll probably notice that your page number is hard up against the dotted 'Footer' line above it. After inserting your page number, your cursor should be live in front of it. The most consistent way to format your footer is to go to the **Footer style** in your **Styles Pane**, choose **Modify → Format → Paragraph → 12 pt Before**. (And click OK as needed to apply, of course!)

To move your page number down a bit, click in front of the **Paragraph mark** (¶) below the number and hit **Delete** to remove the blank line below the page number. Your page number should now be reasonably close to centred in the gap between the end of the text and the bottom of the page.

Point at the greyed out text area of your document and double click on it. This will close the footer and allow you to continue editing your story. Alternatively, click the cross above **Close Header and Footer** on the **Insert** ribbon.

It is possible that the page count of your document has increased due to the extra space taken up by the footer. Have you noticed a change?

Quickly insert a header

Now that we have our pages numbered, we're also going to remind the reader of the title of the book that they're reading. If a page should ever come away from the book, having the title of the book on at least every second page will help the finder know which book it came from. It's also great marketing – if someone is reading over someone else's shoulder on the train or bus, they will be able to see what the book is and go buy their own copy!

Again, we have a couple of choices here, but the quickest way to insert our header is to point at the footer or header area of our document and double-click, thus activating our header and footer areas. Now that the header and footer areas are active, scroll up or down if necessary and click in one of the header spaces.

To make the book a little smarter, we're going to have the author's name on the left hand (even numbered) pages, and the book's name on the right hand (odd numbered) pages. To do this, you will need to place a check in the box against **Different Odd & Even Pages** in the Header and Footer menu under the Design tab.

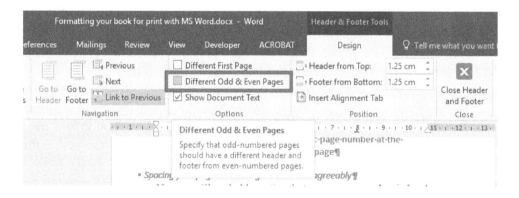

Figure 29: Specify a different header for each of the odd and even pages

If you look at your document you will now see that your headers are labelled **Odd Page Header** and **Even Page Header**.

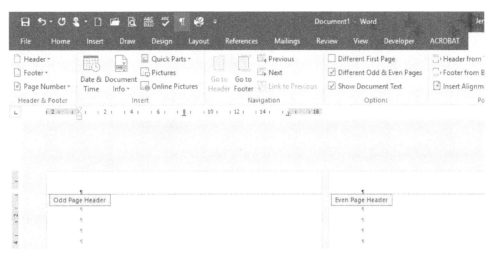

Figure 30: Odd and Even Page Header labels

These may not show on the left and right hand side of the screen the way you would expect in a book, so don't fall into the trap of thinking that odd pages will be on the left. In the print version, they should always be on the right!

The next thing to do is type *Paris Portingale* in the **Even Page Header** space and *Roast Beef, Cheese, Love and Pickles* in the **Odd Page Header** space.

Notes:

_____

_____

_____

_____

_____

_____

_____

_____

_____

_____

Formatting your page headers a little more agreeably

So now we have the author name and the book title in the headers, but they are probably both left aligned, which means that the book name will always appear near the spine of the book while the author name will always appear towards the far left hand side of the double page spread. To my mind, this is kind of ugly, so we're going to format these headers a little more tastefully.

We'll start with the title, *Roast Beef, Cheese, Love and Pickles*. We could centre it, like the page numbering, but let's be different. Click on a header with *Roast Beef, Cheese, Love and Pickles* in it, then go to **Home** on your menu, and click the **right align box** to move *Roast Beef, Cheese, Love and Pickles* to the far right hand side of the page. Notice how *Paris Portingale* stays on the left hand side?

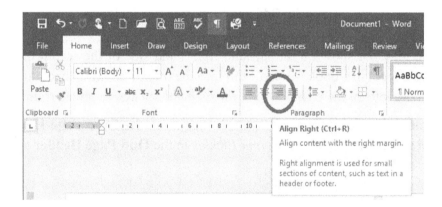

Figure 31: Right align the header for the book's title

If you were to try aligning the author's name by modifying the Header Style, you would find that both the author's name and the book title would align to the same position on the page.

Now point at *Paris Portingale* and triple-click to highlight those words. Then, either from the quick formatting pop-up menu, or from your **Home** menu on the ribbon, choose *I* to italicise the author's name.

Next, highlight the title of the book (point at *Roast* or *Beef* and triple-click to quickly highlight the whole paragraph) and on your **Home** menu, choose the drop arrow next to your Capitalisation options (**Aa** button) and then choose

UPPERCASE to change the header to ROAST BEEF, CHEESE, LOVE AND PICKLES.

Now point at **Header** in your **Styles Pane** and choose **Modify → Format → Paragraph → After: 12 pt**. Click **OK**, then **OK** to close and implement.

Check that there are no empty paragraphs below either the author's name or the book's title. If there are, then delete them. Your two headers should be in alignment as should the first line of text at the top of each left and right hand page.

Point at the main text of your document and double-click to close your header and footer.

Notes:

_____

_____

_____

_____

_____

Use Print Preview to check your formatting work

The great thing about Word's **Print Preview** is that if you're formatting for left and right hand pages, Print Preview will show them to you as they should fall when they're printed in a book.

The quickest way to Print Preview is by clicking the magnifying glass in your **Quick Access Toolbar**. The alternative is to click **File → Print** and wait for the preview to load. If you can only see one page in the preview, reduce the magnification using the slider at the bottom right hand side of your screen. Or, hold down Ctrl and scroll forward or backwards on your mouse wheel to adjust the magnification.

How does the book look? Is page 1 page simply a title page with a header and page number and name of the book? Is it a right hand page with no left hand page opposite? Does each chapter then start on a new page?

And now the big one: Do you have page numbers at the foot of the even numbered pages? No? Me neither. Or perhaps you have them on the even pages and not the odd pages? So where did they go, huh?

Well, we inserted the footers, the page numbers, before we inserted the headers. But before we inserted the headers, we chose the option to have **Different Odd & Even Pages** in the Header and Footer menu. This immediately deleted our even (or perhaps odd) page footers.

Reinsert missing footers

The missing footers are easily restored. First, close **Print Preview** (click the **Back arrow** at the top left hand side of your screen) to return to your document.

Point at any existing footer (page number) in your document and double-click to activate the footers (and headers). Use your mouse to highlight the page number then right-click and **Copy.** Scroll to the next page or the one before, place your cursor in the empty footer, then right-click and **Paste** the footer using the first formatting option **Keep Source Formatting**.

Now highlight and delete any extra space inserted *after* the new page number to keep these numbers at the same level on the page as the numbers on the opposite page.

Check your insertions using Print Preview

Now go back to **Print Preview** and check to ensure that you have page numbers on both sides of your document, all the way through, and that they're at the same height/level on the page. You may find that you have an extra page in your document due to the extra line's space added in the footer on your even numbered pages. Save your file.

Notes:

5. Title pages and 'front matter'

Learning aims of this chapter:

- Making the document look more like a book

- Working with Section Breaks as opposed to Page Breaks

- Adjusting Header and Footer automation

The initial pages of your book

Every book should have some form of title page to make it evident what the book is about, what it's called and/or who it's by. Following the title page, on the left hand side, we generally have an 'imprint' page which tells us who the publisher is, a bit more about the author and the book itself, where the book is registered, who did the illustrations, designed the cover etc. The imprint page will also carry a copyright notice informing the reader of any allowable uses or restrictions on use, and may also carry a disclaimer. Sometimes the disclaimer will be on a page of its own.

In the past, credit would be given to the typesetter who would also often detail the types (fonts) and sizes used in laying out the book. With computer layout, we don't tend to do that these days, although there is no law against it.

Following the imprint page we might have a dedication page, then perhaps a blank page on the back of that, then maybe a Foreword, a Precis or an Introduction. If we want the reader to be able to navigate the book, then we might also have a Table of Contents.

There are no real hard and fast rules, other than that the title page goes on the right hand side and the imprint page generally goes on the left hand side. At

IndieMosh we have our own standard format but we also adapt to the individual author's needs.

Setting up introductory pages for *Roast Beef*

When we print preview *Roast Beef*, the title page is on the right hand side (good) but Chapter 1 falls on the left hand side of the book. We have no imprint page and no navigation (table of contents).

Although this is a small book, we're going to insert a Table of Contents so that you can get a feel for how it works and what you can do with it.

Use a Section Break to separate the main body of the book from the front matter

When we separated the chapters we used a simple page break to force each chapter to start on the next page. However, it would be nice if Chapter 1 started on a right hand page. Because we don't want to have to specifically keep count of the pages before Chapter 1, we're going to use the features of Word's **Section Break** function: we're going to insert a Section Break which forces the next section to always start on an odd numbered (right hand) page. This means that regardless of the number of pages prior to Chapter 1, or what we add or delete from now on, Word will force Chapter 1 to always start on a right hand page, even if it means inserting a blank page on the left.

You should still have your paragraph marks turned on. If not, turn them on now (see *Show paragraph marks ...* on page 41, under *Tidy up unwanted line breaks ...*), and place your cursor at the start of the empty line at the top of page 2, where Part 1 starts. If there is no empty line there, press **Enter** to create one, then click on the empty line and format it as Story style. On your ribbon, go to **Layout** then choose **Breaks → Odd Page**. You will notice that Part 1 now starts on page 3, and that there is no page 2.

Open your **Print Preview** and see how this looks. If you've got it right, the title page should still be on the right hand side, and on the back of that should be a blank, unnumbered page, then Part 1 should start on page 3. It's starting to look a *little* like a real book now, isn't it?

Insert an imprint page

Exit Print Preview and scroll to the title page. As you still have your paragraph marks showing, you should notice two sets of dashed lines sharing the line underneath the title. The first half of the line will be single dashes, and the second half of the line a double dashed line. The single dashed line is the simple page break we inserted when we first started separating the parts of the book and the double dashed line represents the **Odd Page Section Break** we inserted just now.

You'll want to keep both. You can have page breaks within a section and we want that – we want to separate the title page from what comes next – so place your cursor between the two sets of dashes and press **Enter**. Your Section Break should now be sitting at the top of the next page.

Go to **Print Preview** again and see the effect this has had on your document. If you've got it right, then the blank page on the back of the title page will now have a number on it (2) and be carrying a header of *Paris Portingale*. This is because you have now told Word to add a page after the title page, so it no longer needs to include a forced blank page to ensure Part 1 sits on the right hand side. So it has deleted the forced blank page, leaving Part 1 still starting on the right. Clever, huh? Close Print Preview to return to your document.

Fill in some imprint page data

Imprint pages differ from book to book, from publisher to publisher, so we're going to place some standard text in here, just to help *Roast Beef* look more like a real book. **Place** your cursor at the top of the page, right in front of the **Section Break** and perhaps hit **Enter** a couple of times to move the Section Break down the page a little. Then **place** your cursor back at the top of the page, and type after me (ignoring the font and styling I've used below – that's just to make it easier for you to differentiate what you need to type from the rest of the text) ...

Published by My Publishing Company

PO Box 123

MyTown MyState 12345

mypubco.com

First Edition © Paris Portingale 2010

Leave a blank line then continue typing:

> The right of Paris Portingale to be identified as the author of this work has been asserted by him in accordance with the Copyright Amendment (Moral Rights) Act 2000.
>
> Cataloguing-in-Publication entry is available from the National Library of Australia: http://www.nla.gov.au/

Leave another blank line then continue typing:

> Title: → →Roast Beef
>
> Author: →Portingale, Paris
>
> Subject: →Fiction; Romance
>
> ISBNs: →12345 (paperback)
>
>   →98765 (epub)
>
>   →13579 (mobi)

Leave one more blank line then type:

> All rights reserved. Except as permitted under the Australian Copyright Act 1968 (for example, fair dealing for the purposes of study, research, criticism or review) no part of this publication may be reproduced, stored in a retrieval system, or transmitted in any form or by any means, electronic, mechanical, photocopying, recording or otherwise, without written permission of the publisher and author.

Your typing *should* come out in Story style, but if not, then highlight it all and click Story style to temporarily format it as such.

You may also notice that the National Library hyperlink will automatically underline and become a live link. Don't worry about that for this exercise.

Notes:

_____

_____

_____

_____

_____

_____

_____

_____

_____

_____

Format your imprint data

Create an Imprint style for your Imprint page

The Style which was automatically applied to the imprint page won't necessarily be what you want. Depending on how you formatted the rest of the book and how your version of Word is set up, you will probably find that the text on your Imprint page is in the Story style, or else it's in the Normal style – the same style for every new document that you open in Word. And it's feasible that it didn't all fit on the page.

It's nice to have a little control over our imprint page, so highlight all the imprint text and choose **New Style** from your **Styles pane** (by clicking the *A_A icon at the foot of the Styles pane).

Call the new style **Imprint**, it needs to be a **Paragraph** style, base it on **Normal** style, with **Imprint** style following, and set it at **Times New Roman 11 pt, left aligned** (*not* justified). Under the **Format tab** at the lower left hand side of the dialogue box, choose **Paragraph** and ensure that your paragraphs are set to **0 pt Before** and **6 pt After**, with **Single line spacing**.

Reduce selected line spacing

Now that you've reduced the imprint 'guff' (yes, that's a technical term in my book!) to 11 pt, it should all fit on the one page. However, there's a bit of spacing that could be better, such as in the publishing company's address – that 6pt After is spreading it right out, as there is a 'paragraph break' at the end of each line.

What would look better would be if the two lines of the publisher's address sat closer together. To achieve this, place your cursor after PO Box 123, hold your **Shift** button down and press **Enter**. This will place a manual line break (also known as a soft break) at the end of the line. It tells Word that the two lines belong together, but to show them separately.

However, they're still not together, are they? Press **Delete** to remove the blank line now sitting between them and watch as PO Box 123 and MyTown MyState 12345 snap together.

Now rinse and repeat at the end of the ISBN lines to keep that data together.

The soft line breaks here may make a mess of your indents. If that's the case, go to the second line (for the epub) and insert or delete tab marks as necessary so that the start of the placeholder number lines up with the one above, then repeat for the mobi ISBN line. You may find that this automatically adds a tab mark to the paperback ISBN line. If so, then delete that and the whole lot should start to line up like little soldiers.

Notes:

Create a little white space for certain data to 'breathe'

Now that we've condensed the address a little, let's isolate it from the more legal bits about Paris and his book. Click at the end of mypubco.com and press **Enter** to create a blank line between the address and Paris' credit.

If you can't see your Section Break clearly at the bottom of the page, if it's sitting on the same line as the words 'publisher and author', then place your cursor to the right of the full-stop after 'author' and press **Enter** to move the Section Break to a line of its own.

Turn off your paragraph marks for a moment and you'll see that the imprint guff is sitting towards the top of the page. Place your cursor in front of *Published by My Publishing Company* at the top, and press **Enter** to move everything down one line. There, that's looking a little neater now, isn't it?

Turn your paragraph marks back on so that you can see what's happening elsewhere in the document.

Hide or remove active hyperlinks

When you type your imprint data out, you may find that the National Library's hyperlink (URL or website address) gets activated automatically the moment you hit **Enter**. (By 'activated', I mean that it suddenly turns blue and becomes underlined.) As we're currently working on the print book, we don't want any hyperlinks to be underlined – it makes them hard to read – so we need to remove this underline and return the text to black.

As we intend to use this manuscript as the basis for the ebook, we want to leave the hyperlink 'live' but format it so that it's easy to read in the print version. To do this, highlight the hyperlink, and click on **Imprint** style. This will remove the underlining and the blue, but leave the hyperlink active.

The alternative is to highlight the hyperlink then on the context menu click the **Underline** (U) formatting option to turn it on, then click again to turn it off (this removes the line) and then change the font colour to black.

If you're not creating an ebook from this document, you can remove the hyperlink completely and leave just the text. To do this, point at the hyperlink, right-click and from the context menu choose **Remove Hyperlink**.

What's a mobi, Mum?

In the imprint data, the ISBNs for epub and mobi relate to the ebook versions. Mobi is the Kindle ebook version, which will sell on Amazon only, and epub is the non-Kindle ebook format which will be distributed to non-Amazon retailers such as Apple iBooks, Barnes and Noble, Kobo etc.

Create a Dedication page

Not all books have a Dedication page, but just to help you practise some more page formatting techniques, we're going to introduce one here.

At the foot of the Imprint page, we currently have a Section Break (Odd Page) which means that the next page will be on a right hand or odd page. If we move to the next page, it's the first page of the actual story, and we don't want the Dedication page to be included in that section – it's not part of the story – we want it to be part of the front matter. So **place** your cursor after the last paragraph on the Imprint page, just after the full-stop after '… the publisher and author' and before the Section Break, and **insert** a **Manual Page Break**. You can do this using one of three different methods:

1. Use a shortcut: press **Ctrl+Enter**

2. Go to your ribbon and choose **Insert → Page Break** (on the left hand side of the Insert menu ribbon)

3. Go to your ribbon and choose **Layout → Breaks → Page**.

After inserting this page break, you will now have a blank page with the Section Break (Odd Page) sitting at the top. There should be a blank line above it, created when you created your page break. Place your cursor on the blank line and press **Enter** once so that we're not typing the dedication at the very top of the page.

Now, I wouldn't presume to imagine what sort of dedication Paris might write, so we'll keep this really generic and simple and just type 'To my wife'. Don't add a full-stop afterwards – it's not a proper sentence so doesn't require one, much like a title doesn't require one. Now, it's sitting kind of awkwardly there at the top left hand side of the page, so let's place our cursor in the blank line above and press **Enter** a few times to move it down the page to about one third of the page from the top.

Why one third? In art, there is a 'one-third, two-thirds' rule which suggests that you construct your painting or drawing so that major elements of your work appear at a one-third or two-thirds point on your page or canvas, either from the top or from the side. If you look at many artworks you will notice that the subject matter often doesn't sit front and centre – the horizon will be one third up the page, or perhaps one-third of the way down from the top. The big tree in the landscape will be sitting to the left or the right of centre, about a third of the way in. Not all artworks follow the one-third, two-thirds rule, but now that you know about it, have a look and see how often you can see major elements sitting at one-third and two-third lines and intersections!

So now that we've applied a little artwork to our Dedication, let's apply a little more. At the moment it's sitting to the left hand side of the page, in the same font as the Imprint matter. I am sure Paris' wife is more important to him than that, so let's make it look like he means this dedication!

Move your cursor to the line where you've typed *To my wife*. We'll create a new style called Dedication. If we change any of our other styles, the Dedication won't change.

Bring up your **New Style** box and name your new style **Dedication**. The **Type** should be **Paragraph** and we want it based on **Normal**. The style for following paragraphs doesn't really matter much, but choose **Story**, just in case. Now let's format the text. Choose **Centred** for the alignment, then let's change the font to **Monotype Corsiva**, just to make it look a little more 'handwritten' and we'll increase that font size to **18 pt**.

As you make each of these changes, you should be able to see the effect in the preview field in the middle of the **New Style** dialogue box.

Click **OK** when you're done and see how your dedication looks now. Much nicer, hey?

If you **Print Preview** your document now, you will see that your Dedication sits on the right hand page, and when you go to the next page, the first page of the story still starts on a right hand page, thanks to your Section Break (Odd Page) that's now sitting below *To my wife*.

Notes:

_____

_____

_____

_____

_____

_____

_____

Insert a Table of Contents

For a small book like this, a Table of Contents (ToC) isn't necessary, but you do need to know how to insert one and how to format it.

We don't want the ToC sitting on the Dedication page, so place your cursor after 'To my wife' and enter *two* manual page breaks. (The quickest way is using **Ctrl+Enter** twice.) We need two because we want a blank page behind the Dedication and the ToC on the right hand page.

So why not use another Section Break (Odd Page)? We can, and in some instances, perhaps in a text or reference book with a lot of different front matter, you would. But the more section breaks you have, the more you need to do to control them. With Roast Beef, we really only have two parts: the front matter and the story. And everything in the front matter will follow similar rules, so we can just use a couple of simple page breaks here.

Now that you have two blank pages, place your cursor at the top of the second blank page (which should be an odd numbered page) and then press **Enter** once to insert a blank line. You should now have two paragraph marks above the Section Break (Odd Page) marker and your cursor should be to the left of the second one. I have discovered from years of experience that placing a ToC at the very top of a page, without a blank line ahead of it, limits me in my ability to do things with it. You can always delete the blank line later if you don't want or need it.

Now that we know where we're putting our ToC, we need to insert it. Word is marvellous for this – it will draw the ToC from every line we've formatted as Heading 1. And if we had lower-level headings (such as chapter sub-divisions) formatted as Heading 2 or Heading 3, it would pull those through as well.

To create your ToC, on your ribbon go to **Reference → Table of Contents → Automatic Table 1** – the first option – to keep it simple and clean.

Voila! You should now have a list of five parts with their page numbers. If you point at any one of these, press **Ctrl** and then **left-click** with your mouse, you should be able to jump straight to that part of the document.

Notes:

_____

_____

_____

_____

_____

_____

_____

The value of a ToC

Even in a small document like this, where you probably don't need a ToC for the published work, it's still a good idea to create a ToC temporarily, just to ensure that everything's headed up correctly. You can easily delete it once you're happy your document has been correctly formatted.

Have a look at the ToC you've just created. Unless you picked it up earlier and changed it yourself, you'll find that we have two parts with the same number, and that the final part will need to have its number changed!

If you discover errors such as these in your ToC, *don't* make the changes there – they won't be sticky (yes, another technical term!). Instead, make the change to the heading in the document itself and update the ToC to draw the updated heading through.

Updating your ToC after changes in the manuscript

Point at **Part 3 – Johanna** in your ToC and press **Ctrl-Click** to be taken directly to that heading. Change the **3** to a **4**.

Now scroll down to **Part 4 – The Car Park** and change the **4** to a **5**.

While this updates the manuscript, it doesn't update the ToC. **Return** to the ToC, **point** at it, **right click** and choose **Update Field** then **Update entire table**. Your ToC should now show the parts with correct numbering.

Format your ToC

For the moment, your ToC looks okay, but it could be a little prettier. Point at your ToC, **right-click** and choose **Edit Field**. In the dialogue box, under **Categories:** select **Index and Tables**, then highlight **TOC** in the section below that. Ensure that there's a tick in the box in the lower right-hand side of the dialogue box to **Preserve formatting during updates** then click **Table of Contents** towards the centre top of the dialogue box.

We want our readers to be able to find the sections easily, so ensure that there are ticks in the following boxes:

- Show page numbers
- Right align page numbers

Now let's click **Modify** and change the font, size and spacing of our ToC entries. When the Style box opens, **TOC 1** is automatically highlighted. As we've done nothing fancy in the text, this will relate to Heading 1 – the style we applied to each of the Part headings. Click **Modify** to open the Modify Style box for this part of the ToC. Change the font to **Bernard MT Condensed**, to match Paris' branding and the font size to **9**. Click **Format → Paragraph** and change the spacing to **12 pt After**. Click **OK, OK, OK** until you're done, and watch the ToC change as you close your dialogue box. If prompted to replace the ToC, choose **Yes**.

Notes:

_____

_____

_____

_____

_____

_____

Format your ToC heading to match your other headings

For starters, the title *Contents* is pretty ugly in comparison with the chapter headings, so let's format it to match the other headings in the document. But first off, we need to recall the settings for the other headings.

On your **Styles pane**, point at **Heading 1** and left-click on the drop-down arrow to bring up the context menu, then left-click on **Modify** to bring up the **Modify Style** dialogue box. Have a look at the formatting you've set and take note of the main points:

- Font: Berlin Sans FB

- Size: 16 pt

- Alignment: Centred

- Paragraph spacing Before: 24 pt, After 12 pt

Click **Cancel** to close the dialogue box when you've finished.

Point and left-click once anywhere on the word **Contents** at the top of your ToC. Be careful not to highlight any particular letters – just click somewhere in the word. Now look at your **Styles pane** – at the bottom you should see a new style called **TOC Heading** and it should be highlighted now that you've clicked on the word **Contents**. Point at the **TOC Heading** style and left-click on the drop arrow to bring up the context menu, then left-click on **Modify** to bring up the **Modify Style** dialogue box. (If yours shows as **TOC 1**, then click on **TOC Heading** to format it as the TOC Heading style.)

The dialogue box will show you that the style is called **TOC Heading** and that it's a **Paragraph** style based on **Heading 1** and that the following style should be **Normal**. However, unless a miracle has occurred, it will look nothing like **Heading 1**!

Notes:

_____

_____

_____

_____

_____

_____

_____

_____

Now we've made the decision that the ToC heading should be the same as the Part headings (and by 'we' I mean 'I'), let's change the fields to match Heading 1 as noted above. Remember that to change your Paragraph spacing (24 pt Before and 12 pt After) you will need to click on the **Format** button at the bottom left of the dialogue box and choose **Paragraph** from the pop-up list.

Close each context menu as you complete the necessary changes and click **OK** to finalise your **TOC Heading** format. Watch it snap into the centre of the line in the same font and size as the Part headings.

Print Preview and check that the ToC sits on a right hand page and that there is a blank page to its left.

The quick way to update your ToC Heading

Now that you've practised changing your ToC, there is a quicker way to update the ToC heading. And, indeed, other styles in your manuscript.

First of all, scroll through your document until you reach a page with the beginning of a chapter/part. Click once on a heading which says *Part X – ...* to place your cursor on the heading. This line should have previously been formatted as Heading 1. You don't need to highlight the whole line, just click *in* it somewhere.

Now go to your **Styles pane** and scroll to the bottom, until you see **TOC Heading**. Point to the right hand end of that line to bring up the **Modify** drop arrow. The first option in the context menu will be **Update TOC Heading to Match Selection**. If you choose this option, then your ToC heading should then adopt Heading 1 formatting. Scroll back to your ToC, around page 5 of your document, and see if *Contents* now has the same style as the rest of your headings.

If you have more than one level of headings, then you can choose something other than Heading 1 to update your TOC Heading to, if you'd rather.

Back to the title page

Format your title

Now that we have our introductory pages laid out, it's time to make our first page – our title page – stand out. We'll start by creating a new style called **Book Name** based on **Normal**. Word does have an inbuilt style called Book Title, but I have always found it hard to work with and so prefer to create my own.

The first thing to do is click anywhere on the line with *Roast Beef* in it and call up the **New Style** dialogue box. Call the new style **Book Name**, and, to be consistent with the chapter or part headings, set the font as **Berlin Sans FB**, but make it **26 pt** and centred so that it 'lands' on the page. Ensure that paragraph formatting is **0 pt Before** and **0 pt After**, with **no indents** and (**none**) for **Special**.

Roast Beef, Cheese, Love and Pickles

Format your author name

Now, Paris put his name at the end of his document, not at the top, so you'll need to type it on the title page, below the title. But Paris has a particular branding for his name: his first name is in all capitals, but his last name isn't, and his names appear on separate lines. So type **PARIS** in capitals on one line, press **Enter** then type **Portingale** in sentence case on the next line.

We now need to create two styles to format his name on the title page: **Author First** and **Author Last**.

Click on **PARIS** and create a new **Author First** style using:

- Bernard MT Condensed 16 pt Centred

- Paragraph spacing (under Format) of 0 pt Before and 0 pt After, with Single line spacing, with No indents and (none) for Special:

PARIS

Now click on **Portingale** and create an **Author Last** style using:

- Bernard MT Condensed 20 pt Centred

- Paragraph spacing (under Format) of 0 pt Before and 0 pt After, with No indents and (none) for Special.

- Line spacing, change Single to Multiple and type 0.9 into the box, to bring the two lines a little closer together:

Portingale

What you have now should look like this:

PARIS
Portingale

That's almost right, but we need to insert five blank spaces *in front of* PARIS so that it moves along to the correct place:

PARIS
Portingale

This is not perfect – it's not *exactly* the same as we could get if we were using InDesign, say – but it's pretty darn close and no one's going to notice that it's not spot on. So long as we give the *impression* of the branding, then most people won't even realise it's not quite 100%.

And this is something important to remember in self publishing – work hard to get it as good as you can, but remember that at the end of the day, perfection is an illusion. You're after good quality, not a nervous breakdown!

Also, it's publishing, not brain surgery – no one's going to die. Unless you're writing a book on brain surgery and you leave out something important. But I digress …

Space your title and author name out

What you'll have now is this big, fancy text on the page, just sitting there in the middle. But it doesn't really look like a title page, does it?

First up, we need to get the title sitting about one third of the way down the page.

Go to your Dedication page and use your cursor to **highlight** every empty line *above* the dedication. Then **right-click** and **Copy**. Return to your title page, **highlight** every blank line above *Roast Beef*, then **right-click** and **Paste**. What you should have achieved was to place the exact same spacing from the Dedication page above the title so that *Roast Beef* and the dedication both appear at the same distance from the top of the page.

Now click in front of *PARIS* and press **Enter** once to create a blank line if none already exists. If there is a blank line (or more) between *Roast Beef* and *PARIS*, then place your cursor there, highlighting every blank line if there's more than one.

Now **click** on **Story** style so every blank line is the same line height and font size.

After doing that, just click in front of the first blank line and start pressing **Enter** until Paris' name moves to the very bottom of the page. You may need to delete any blank lines after *Portingale* to allow it to move to the bottom without creating a blank page after it.

You should now have a title page which looks something like this but, without the border:

Roast Beef, Cheese,
Love and Pickles

PARIS
Portingale

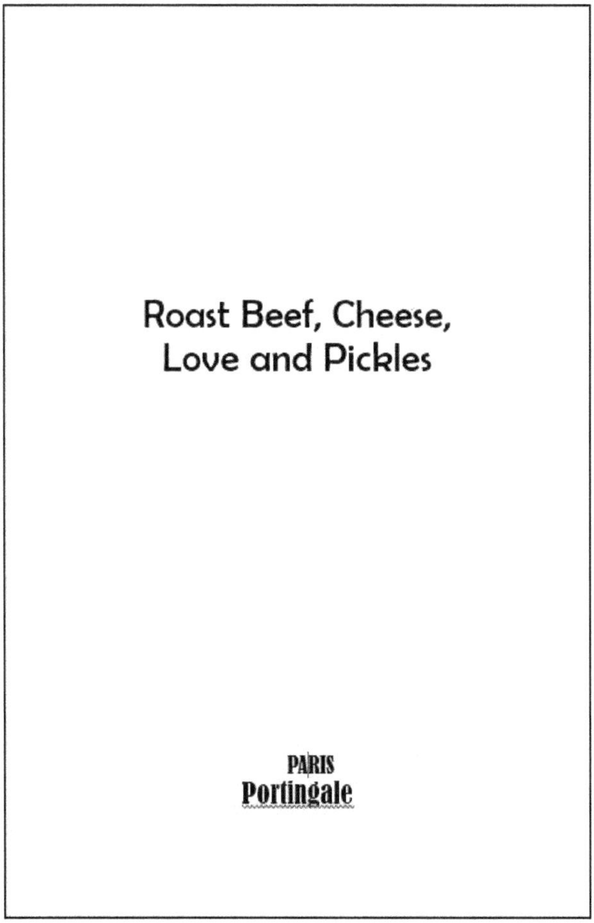

Figure 32 : Your title page should look something like this, but without the border. You may find the first line of your title breaks after 'Love' rather than after 'Cheese'.

Notes:

_____

_____

_____

_____

_____

_____

_____

_____

_____

Getting the headers and footers right

When you inserted your page numbering, it probably started with the very first page of the book – the title page – and continued from there. Normally, the initial pages, the 'guff' pages, don't take the same numbering as the rest of the book. If these pages are to be numbered, we usually use Roman numerals (i.e. i, ii, iii, iv, v, vi, etc.). In a novel, it's usually not necessary to number these pages at all, unless you're having a Foreword (not a Forward!) and other material, so we're going to remove all page numbering from the initial pages and make Page 1 the very first page of *Part 1 – Graham*.

Delete page numbers from initial pages

Go to *Part 1* and double-click on any of the footers (page numbers) in *Part 1 – Graham* to activate the headers and footers.

When you look closely at the footer it will have two labels: **Even Page Footer – Section 2** (or **Odd Page Footer – Section 2**) on one side and **Same as Previous** on the right hand side.

What we need to do is 'break' the link between the headers and footers in Section 2 (the body of the document) and Section 1 (the guff) so that we can start numbering the story itself from page 1. To do this:

- Look at your menu ribbon and you should see that the text **Link to Previous** is highlighted. **Left click** on this once to break the link. It should now no longer be greyed out.

- Now move your cursor to the next footer (if you were on an even page, you now need to move to an odd one, and vice-versa), and **repeat the above process**.

- Now move your cursor to the heading on that page and again, **left click** once to remove the link to the headers in Section 1.

- Then move to the next page and **repeat the process**.

- Now scroll up to the title page or the imprint page and start deleting page numbers and headers. You should only have to delete one of each from any of the odd numbered pages and one of each from any of the even numbered pages.

- Double-click on the body of the document to close the headers and footers, or click the red cross above **Close Header and Footer** in the ribbon. When you return to your document, you should have no headers or footers in your document until you reach *Part 1 – Graham*.

Notes:

_____

_____

_____

_____

_____

_____

_____

The six Header and Footer options available

When working with headers and footers, you have six discrete spaces to label your pages in each section:

1. A first page header
2. A first page footer
3. An even page header
4. An even page footer
5. An odd page header
6. An odd page footer

Some people only take two options – a header (the same on every page) and a footer, usually a page number (the same on every page), but if you insert a section break between each chapter, which is often useful in a non-fiction book where the headers can help remind the reader where they're up to, you can format:

- the first page of each chapter to have no header
- the first page of each chapter to have a page number
- the even page header of each chapter to take the book's title
- the odd page of each chapter to take the chapter name
- the even footer to show the page number on the left
- the odd page footer to show the page number on the right.

Notes:

Page numbering conventions for novels

Most novels show no page numbers for the early pages, and simply start with '1' being the first page of the story itself. Novels with a table of contents may sometimes show separate page numbers in Roman numerals (i, ii, iii, ix etc) for pages with content, but usually no page numbers are shown on the title pages or imprint or dedication pages.

The normal standard for the first page of the story itself would be to have a page number but no header. What do you have on the first page of the body of the book, the first page of Section 2? If you have no page number and need to have one showing, or if you have a pager header and wish to suppress it, double-click in either the header or footer to open the Header and Footer ribbon.

Delete the Header from page 1

You can't delete the header from page 1 alone – doing so will remove it from all odd numbered pages for the rest of the book! What you need to do is *suppress* it. So **click** in the header field if you haven't done so already, and on the **Header and Footer** ribbon **check the box** which says **Different First Page**. This will delete the header. Should you want a different header on the first page of a section, you can type in whatever you want. But in this instance we don't want anything, so we'll just leave it blank.

Insert a page number on page 1

If the page number isn't showing on page 1, then click in the footer and on the Header and Footer ribbon, **uncheck** the box which says **Different First Page**. This should then allow the page number to appear on the first page of *Part 1 – Graham*.

Setting the page numbers to start at the right number

If the page number at the foot of Part 1 isn't a '1' (and it probably won't be), then we need to tell Word to start counting from this page.

With your cursor still in the footer, go to the left hand end of your **Header and Footer** ribbon, click the drop arrow next to **Page Number** and towards the bottom choose **Format Page Numbers...**

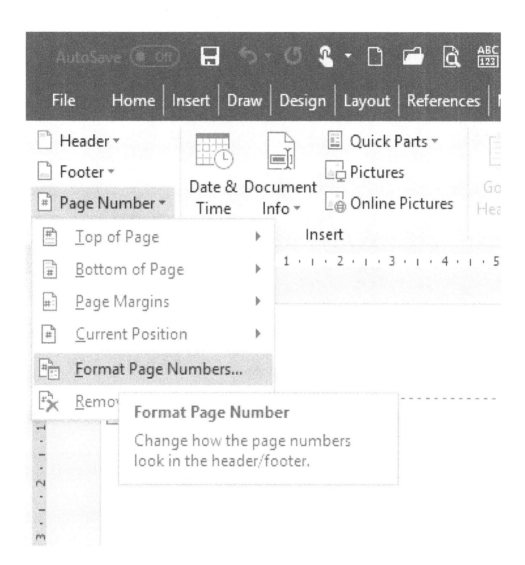

Figure 33 : Accessing the Format Page Numbers menu

When the dialogue box opens, make sure that the choice of numbering at the top is **1, 2, 3** and then lower down click **Start at** and ensure that **1** is the number in the box.

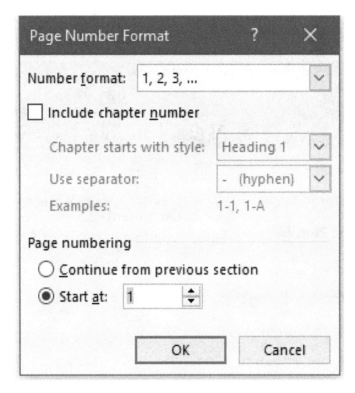

Figure 34: Setting the starting page number for that section

Click **OK** to return to your footer – you should see that it's now a 1 – and scroll to the next two pages to make sure that they're showing a 2 and a 3 respectively. If that's the case, then the rest of the document should be fine as there are no more section breaks. **Double-click** on the text to close your header and footer menu.

Save your file if you haven't already done so.

Set Roman numerals for your initial pages

If you want Roman numerals on your initial pages, then **double-click** in the header or footer of one of the initial pages to activate the headers and footers. **Click** in your preferred spot for page numbers, and **repeat the process in Figs 30 and 31 above** to set the page number style for that section, making sure to choose **Roman numerals** from the drop list for **Number format**.

If you only want Roman numerals on your ToC page onwards, say, and not your title page etc., then insert a **New Page section break** (Layout → Breaks) prior to the page where you want numbering to start. **Click** in the header or footer where you *do* want the numbers, **uncheck Link to previous** in your ribbon menu, then delete the numbering from where you don't want it.

Notes:

6. Let's add some gravy

Learning aims of this chapter:

- The effects of different page sizes
- Looking at the page from a basic design point of view
- Working with vertical justification, widows and orphans
- Using Find and Replace to wrangle and tidy little things

Quick summary of where we're at right now

Now that you've been through the initial formatting process, you should have a bit of a handle on the main tools of the formatting trade:

- Styles pane
- Styles and the ability to modify them
- Navigation pane
- Find and replace function

In this section we'll look at using these in a bit of depth to spit and polish your manuscript a bit more. If you're remotely creative, you should find this quite fun!

Getting an appropriate page size

When you first start laying out a book, you won't really know how many pages it's going to take up. It's important to only use as many pages as necessary so as to keep printing costs down. And, if you keep the page count down, you'll keep the weight down, which might also help with shipping costs.

Naturally, we still need to give the reader a pleasant reading experience. There is nothing worse than fonts so small and lines packed so tightly that the reader gets a headache or keeps losing their place on their page. (Think airport novels.) But there's also no point in releasing a novel for adults in a font so large and line spacing so loose that it looks like a children's story, so balance is the key.

Create a new file for a smaller page size

Make a note of the page count of your current version of *Roast Beef* in the 6 x 9 inch set up. What we're going to do now is reduce the page size to 5 x 8 which is a comfy little single-hand size for smaller books. But we'll leave the file you've been working on 'as is' so that you can see the difference.

Ensure that you have *Roast Beef for Print* (not the original *Roast Beef* file) open on your screen, choose **File → Save as** and save it as **Roast Beef for Print 5 x 8**. This action will close the original file and leave the new file titled **Roast Beef for Print 5 x 8** open on your screen so you can continue working.

Notes:

_____

_____

_____

_____

_____

_____

_____

_____

_____

_____

_____

_____

Change the page size

Go to **Layout** → **Page Setup** and click on the arrow at the bottom right hand corner of the Page Setup section.

Click on the **Paper tab**, on the **Page Setup** menu.

Just under the **Paper Size** option, enter **5** (inches) or **12.70** (cm) in the **Width** field (depending on how your version of Word is set up – whether it's Imperial or Metric) and then **8** (inches) or **20.32** (cm) in the **Height** field.

Towards the bottom of the dialogue box, make sure the words **Whole Document** show in the **Apply to** field. If they don't, then click the drop arrow and choose **Whole Document**.

Click **OK** and watch *Roast Beef for Print 5 x 8* suddenly resize. Save the file in its new format.

Now go to **Print Preview** and have a look at the document. You may find that the text on your title or imprint page is flowing over to the next page, forcing your Dedication over onto a left hand page, or even the page after. We'll fix this next.

What should work, though, is that each **Part** should still start on a new page, and Part 1 should still start on a right hand, odd numbered page, regardless of whether or not your imprint page is now running to two pages.

Notes:

_____

_____

_____

_____

_____

_____

Fix things to look good on the new page size

Title page

Close **Print Preview** and go to your title page, placing your cursor anywhere on the title. It probably looks a bit big now that the page is smaller, so in your Styles pane, point at the **Book name** style, click the drop arrow at the right and choose **Modify...** When the dialogue box opens, change the title size to **24 pt** and click **OK**.

Looking at the author name, it seems a bit heavy on such a small page, doesn't it? In your **Styles pane**, point at the **Author First** style, click the drop arrow at the right and choose **Modify...** Change the font size to **12 pt**. Then move across to the Font colour box and, rather than Automatic, change the font colour to a medium-dark grey, making a note of which grey you picked. Click **OK**.

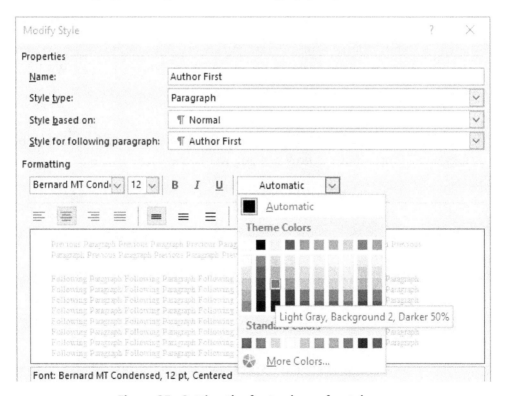

Figure 35 : Setting the font colour of a style

Now point at **Author Last** in your Styles pane, click the drop arrow and choose **Modify…** and reduce that font size to **16 pt** and make that font colour the same shade of grey as **Author First** style. It should now appear something like this, clear but not overwhelming:

PARIS

Portingale

Imprint page

Scroll to your Imprint page and in your **Styles pane**, point at the **Imprint** style, choose **Modify...**, change the font size to **10 pt** (from 11 pt) and click **OK**.

Does the text fit on one page now? If not, then maybe you just need to delete the last paragraph break so that the page break sits at the end of the last line of text. Or maybe modify the font again to 9 pt. You can also type over the font size manually, and make it 9.5 pt.

Body of the story

Now that the page size is so much smaller, the text might look a bit large – and there won't be quite so many words to a line!

Place your cursor somewhere in a normal paragraph, but without highlighting any actual text. On your **Styles pane**, point to **Story** and choose **Modify**. Change the font size to 11 pt and click **OK**. How does this look now? It will have reduced your page count, as well as the font size.

If it still seems a bit large, then consider repeating the process, bringing the main text down to 10 pt.

If that seems too small, repeat the process again, but type 10.5 over the 10 in the font size box and see if that's just right. Sometimes we have to think, 'What would Goldilocks do?'

The first paragraph in each section – formatted as **Story first** – should also changes size accordingly as this style was based on **Story**.

Headers and footers

Now that you've changed the body of the text, the headers and footers will probably look quite large, too. Activate your headers and footers by double-clicking on one or the other.

Click on the drop arrow for the **Footer** style in the **Styles pane** to bring up the **Modify Style** dialogue box. Let's change the footer font to 9 pt – make it smaller than the body of the book. Click **OK**. This should change the font for both left and right pages.

Now click on the **Header** style in the **Styles pane**. Change this to 10 pt, or perhaps 9.5 pt if the body of your book is still at 10 pt. Click **OK**.

Tweak the margins

Now that we've downsized all these things, you may feel that the outer margins are a little large for such a small book. That's okay – again, they're easily fixed!

On your ribbon menu, go to **Layout → Page Setup** and click the drop arrow at the bottom right hand side of the Page Setup section. Click the **Margins** tab and change **Outside** to **0.67** inches or **1.7** cms. Click **OK**.

Again, the text will reflow and it's possible you may even save another page or three!

Notes:

_____

_____

_____

_____

_____

_____

_____

Vertical Justification

If you look closely at a commercially published novel, you will probably notice that the bottom line of each full page sits at the same distance from the bottom edge of the page as the bottom line of the full page opposite. Microsoft Word can help you achieve this.

Applying vertical justification

First of all, click somewhere in the *story* part of the book so that your cursor is *not* sitting in any of the pages *before* Part 1. Then, on your ribbon menu, go to **Layout → Page Setup** and click the drop arrow at the bottom right hand side of the Page Setup section. Click the **Layout** tab and ensure that either **This section** or **This point forward** is showing against the **Apply** option at the bottom of the dialogue box. If it says **Whole document**, then click the drop arrow and change it to **This section** or **This point forward**. We don't want to apply this change to the title, imprint or dedication pages, although you may choose to, depending on the document you're creating.

In the middle of the dialogue box under the Layout tab is a field titled **Vertical alignment** (under the heading **Page**). The default option is **Top**. Click the drop arrow and change it to **Justified**. Click **OK** to close the dialogue box. Close your headers and footers by either double-clicking on the text part of your document, or by clicking the X in the Header and Footer Tools menu.

Fix the last pages of each chapter or section

Head to the last page of Part 1. What you'll see – if there's more than one paragraph on that page – is that the paragraphs are spreading out to fill up the page. They're justifying vertically.

To fix this, place your cursor below the last paragraph and start hitting the **Enter** key until the page break slips over to the top of the next page. (You should still have your paragraph marks turned on.) Once the page break slips to the next page, delete the last paragraph mark/empty paragraph you inserted and watch the page break snap back. The text paragraphs should now be sitting together at the top of the page with no additional space between them.

Rinse and repeat for the other chapters, where necessary.

You will notice that any last page with only one paragraph on it will leave that paragraph at the top of the page, so it will only be the last page where there are two or more paragraphs that you need to insert additional space.

A note on paragraph spacing for when you're formatting for others

When you're fixing the justification at the end of each chapter, it's a good idea to leave this until close to finalisation of the formatting, especially if you're sending the document to the author in stages for approval. Explain that you know these paragraphs are spaced out down the page and that they'll be fixed at the end, as there's no point doing them now as other changes may affect them, and so you'd just be wasting your time fixing them now.

Widows and Orphans

An internet search of 'widows and orphans' will probably provide you with conflicting answers as to which is which, but in short, they are one of:

- the last few words at the end of a paragraph which sit by themselves at the top of the next page

- the first line of a paragraph which has been left stranded at the bottom of a page while the rest of the paragraph sits on the next page

- the last word on a line by itself at the end of a paragraph.

Before computers, these were edited out by the editing team and the author, or manipulated out by the typesetter. In today's world, however, most readers won't notice them. But now you're aware of them, you will!

Scroll through *Roast Beef for Print 5 x 8* and see if you have any single lines at the top or bottom of a page. Or a single word on a line by itself at the end of a paragraph. How do they look? A bit stranded?

When we set up **Story** style we cleared the check box against **Widow/Orphan control**:

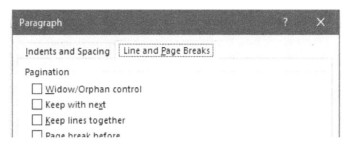

Figure 36 : Widow and Orphan control

Clearing that check box meant that Word will allow paragraphs to break *after* the *first* line or *before* the *last* line. If that box is checked, then Word will keep the first or last two lines of a paragraph together at the top or bottom of a page.

So that you can see the effect of *suppressing* widows and orphans, click to **Modify** your **Story** style. At the bottom of the **Modify Style** dialogue box, click **Format** →**Paragraph**. Click the **Line and Page Breaks** tab and click the **Widow/Orphan control** box. Click **OK** then **OK**.

Now have a look at some of the pages in your document. What you'll find is that where Word can't fit the first two lines of a paragraph on one page, it will move that entire paragraph to the top of the next page. Because we've applied vertical justification to the page, the other paragraphs on the prior page will be spreading out vertically to fill up the space, the way words spread out horizontally to fill up a justified line.

Notes:

If you want to automatically suppress the widows and orphans in your document, then you're faced with either turning off vertical justification so that paragraphs don't get all 'gappy' or else manually editing the text or specific paragraphs so that the gappy paragraphs fill up the page.

Personally, while it's lovely to have widows and orphans suppressed and manuscripts edited to fit, this is the 21st century and most people are more interested in the content. If your book is as error-free as possible and laid out neatly, they'll probably not notice the odd widow or orphan.

So my recommendation is to *allow* widows and orphans – uncheck that **Widow/Orphan control** box in your Story style – and let them land where they land. If they bother you too much, it's probably easier to edit the odd paragraph here and there to tidy the text up. Just bear in mind that fixing one may introduce another on the next page – or three pages further on!

Fix widows, orphans and gappy paragraphs by editing the text

If you've got the patience, you can probably amend the text of a paragraph here or there to fix most widows or orphans. Or if you've suppressed widows and orphans and now have gaps between paragraphs on some pages, again, you'll need to tweak something to get rid of the gaps.

Some people believe that InDesign will allow you to do magical things to fix these issues, but in many cases, it can't do any more than Word – the fix can be applied using the software, but it still has to be found and addressed manually.

For instance, your layout may create a page that allows 28 normal lines of text. But if you've suppressed widows and orphans, and you have a paragraph at the top of a page with three lines, followed by paragraphs of ten, eleven and three lines, that's a total of 27 lines. And that will give you gaps between the paragraphs. You can't bring two lines back from the next page – they won't fit – and you've suppressed widows and orphans, so you can't even have one at the bottom of the page. In this instance, the math doesn't work – you'll have to intervene manually, one way or another.

You can sometimes break a larger paragraph up into two or three paragraphs to force a line over so that it joins up with the others on the next page, or to remove space on a page. Or, you can perhaps join a couple of paragraphs together to bring a line or more back from a following page to help.

The alternative is to rephrase or recast a sentence here or there, or to delete a word or two – especially 'weasel words' – to help bring words or lines back or force them over to the next line or page. If you're going to do this, the two things you need to remember are:

1. If you change the text at all, make sure you re-read the entire paragraph very carefully in case you've introduced an error or accidentally changed the meaning of the sentence or paragraphs.

2. If you're combining or separating paragraphs, make sure that you're still observing any rules applied to the rest of the book regarding which types of paragraph are combined, and which are kept separate.

Notes:

_____

_____

_____

_____

_____

_____

_____

_____

_____

_____

_____

_____

_____

Fix widows, orphans and gappy paragraphs by tweaking character spacing

The other way to fix widows and orphans is to change paragraph spacing.

For single words at the end of a paragraph, you'll need to change the character spacing of that particular paragraph. For lines at the top or bottom of a page, you can change the spacing of any prior paragraph which looks like it will make a difference to the rest of the text.

Triple-click inside a paragraph you wish to change, to quickly highlight the entire paragraph. Then on your menu, choose **Home** and click the drop arrow to the right of **Font**, then click the **Advanced** tab. Click the drop arrow next to **Spacing** and choose **Condensed**, then in the **By** field type **0.1** (pt).

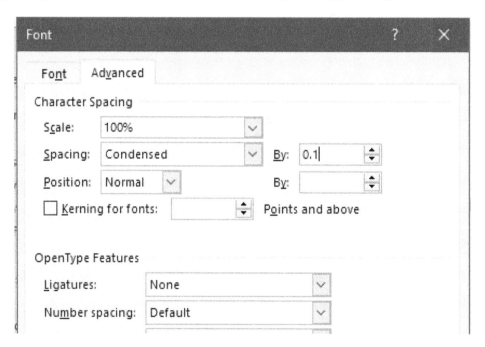

Figure 37: Condensing character spacing to save lines

Click **OK** and see if the difference this makes is enough. If not, repeat the process, changing the figure in the **By** field to **0.2**, then **0.3** and so on, until you get the result you're looking for.

If you have to go past 0.5, you're probably going to find that the text has been condensed too much, in which case you'll need to look for another paragraph to amend.

Once you amend the spacing of any paragraph, you'll notice in your Styles pane that Word has added a new subsidiary style to the main style of that paragraph.

As you work, you might end up with several new subsidiary styles there – each for a different measurement to condense the text spacing by. This makes it easier – you can click in any paragraph and then try an existing subsidiary style to see if it will be enough to fix that particular paragraph, rather than having to go through the whole **Font → Advanced → Condensed → By** process.

The downside of tweaking character spacing

The one thing you'll need to remember, if you're tweaking character spacing, is that you'll have to reverse it all before you export your text to make an ebook, otherwise you'll have an ebook with really inconsistent text spacing, depending on where words fall on the reader's page.

Before you start, save the file as 'for ebook' so that you don't overwrite your print file! You will now have two files – one for print and one for ebooks.

Reversing the spacing adjustments is easily done, though. Point at the drop arrow to the right of any of the subsidiary styles you've made and click **Select All XXX Instance(s)**. Then click on the main style for that paragraph, to change all those paragraphs back to normal spacing in one hit.

If you've applied the style to only selected text in some paragraphs, then do a 'test reversal' in case you lose italics or bold formatting within the paragraph.

Rinse and repeat for each subsidiary style created to tweak the character spacing.

A word of warning

If you do decide to change character spacing, be careful not to lose any instances of **Bold** or *Italics* in any of your text – especially when you're reverting back to a base style. To reduce this risk, highlight and condense only those parts of a paragraph which don't have any special formatting.

Notes:

_____

_____

_____

_____

_____

_____

Tidying up punctuation

Double spacing

In the old days (yep, I'm talking last century – pre-computers!), the standard was to have a double space between each sentence. Many authors still do this without thinking – it's the way we were taught until about the 1980s – but the modern standard is to have a single space between each sentence. The main reason is consistency – it's easier to make sure that there's one space than two – but the other reason is economical. Why waste space? Across a one-hundred thousand word novel, those extra spaces could add several pages, which will, again, add to the cost of printing.

To clean up double spaces in a document, open the **Find and Replace** dialogue box (either from the ribbon or from the drop arrow next to the **Search box** in the **Navigation pane**) and in the **Find** field press your space bar twice. In the **Replace** field press your space bar once.

Click **Find next** and you should be taken to the first instance of a double space in the document. Click **Replace** and Word will replace the double space with a single space and take you to the next double space. Click **Replace** for each double space until Word tells you that there are no more double spaces in the document. Alternatively, click **Replace all** to spare wear and tear on your trigger finger.

Click **OK** then try again. If there was a triple or quadruple space, Word will only have replaced two of the spaces with one, thus reducing that set of spaces by one, so you may need to click **Find** again and run through a couple more times.

Also, Word thinks it's found every instance of whatever it is you're looking for, but sometimes it needs to do a second or even a third pass, just to make sure! So whenever it's finished whatever you're searching, always click 'Find' again until it says it can't find any more.

Notes:

_____

_____

_____

_____

_____

_____

Errant spaces at the start of a line

It's not uncommon for any one of us to accidentally end up with a single space at the start of a line. This can be caused by deleting earlier text or breaking up a paragraph – any number of reasons. But a single space at the start of a line will indent that line just enough to look 'off' when the book prints. They're hard to see onscreen – even with paragraph marks on – so the best thing to do is make sure that they simply don't exist. The next paragraph has a single space before *However* just to illustrate.

 However, some authors use the space bar to indent paragraphs when they're writing. You may have cleaned up someone else's document, but it's always possible that you've left the odd space or three, so here's how to get rid of the pesky little blighters!

In your **Find and Replace** dialogue box, insert a paragraph mark in the **Find** field (**Special → Paragraph Mark** or **^p**) and follow it with a single space. In the **Replace** field simply insert a Paragraph Mark or **^p** *without* any space after.

Click **Find next** and you should be taken to the first instance of a paragraph followed by a single space at the start of a new line. Click **Replace** and the single space should disappear and you should be taken to the next instance.

What's happening is that Word is replacing the paragraph break and the space at the start of the next line with a paragraph break where it already existed, and no space at the start of the next line.

Continue until Word tells you that there are no more instances. Click **OK** then go through the process again, just to make sure you really did get them all. For instance, if there was a line with two spaces at the start, it will now have one space at the start, and Word won't know because it's already checked that line.

Notes:

_____

_____

_____

_____

_____

_____

_____

_____

_____

_____

_____

_____

_____

Ellipsis points

Ellipsis points are three dots (not four, five or six) used in text to either indicate missing text or a trailing off of thought. Although they look like three full-stops, true ellipsis points are a single grouping of consecutive dots which your cursor will jump over as if they were one letter if you press the left and right arrow keys on your keyboard. They should take a single space either side as they represent missing words. In other words, they should not buttress up against the preceding or following words, and nor should they have spaces in between:

This … is correct.

This… is wrong and this…is definitely wrong! As is . . . this!

I have converted some of the ellipsis points in *Roast Beef* to full-stops to help you practise.

The first thing to do is ensure that any dots used are in the correct format, and not three (or more) full-stops. (Some authors will use, three, four, five or more full-stops in a wide variety in the one document – so you have to be able to hunt and gather!)

In your **Find and Replace** box, type three full-stops without spaces between in the **Find** box and click **Find next**. When you find the first set of full-stops, **close** your **Find and Replace** box for the moment.

Look at what's there. Is it just three full-stops? Or are there four or more? What we're going to do is replace all of them with a set of ellipsis points. Then we're going to copy the ellipsis points to our **Replace** box to make the **Find and Replace** task easier.

Place your cursor before the first full-stop. It doesn't matter if there's a space after the word or not – we'll do the spacing separately. On your ribbon, go to **Insert → Symbol**, click the drop arrow below **Symbol** then **More Symbols** to bring up the Symbols dialogue box.

Click the **Special Characters** tab and scroll down the list until you see **Ellipsis**. Click on this then click **Insert**, then close the dialogue box. (Or **double-click** on **Ellipsis** to insert then close your dialogue box.) If you'd prefer a keyboard shortcut, then use **Ctrl-Alt-.** (That's **Control** plus **Alt** plus the **full-stop key**.)

After you insert the ellipsis points, your cursor will be sitting to the right of them, after them. Click the **left arrow** on your keyboard to see how the cursor jumps across all three at once as if they were a single character.

Now highlight the ellipsis points (being careful not to highlight any spaces before or after!) with your mouse and **right-click** then choose **Copy**, or press **Ctrl-C** to copy.

Open your **Find and Replace** box and click in the **Replace** field. **Right-click** and choose **Paste** to place the ellipsis points in the Replace field. You should still have three full-stops in your Find field. If not, then click in the Find field and type three full-stops in.

Click **Find next** and you should get taken to the next set of three full-stops in *Roast Beef for Print 5 x 8*. Click **Replace** to replace them with proper ellipsis points. Repeat until there are no more. (This won't take long – there will only be a couple!)

Notes:

_____

_____

_____

_____

_____

_____

_____

What we're going to do next is replace every set of ellipsis points with a set of ellipsis points with a nonbreaking space attached to the head of them. What this means is that if any of the ellipsis points end up at the end of a line and Word has to justify where to place them, they won't slip to the start of the next line by themselves. Instead, they'll be kept with the preceding word, even if that means that the word and the ellipsis points have to move down to the next line.

With your **Find and Replace** dialogue box still open, copy and paste the ellipsis points from the **Replace** field into the **Find** field. In the **Replace** field, click to place your cursor immediately **in front** of the ellipsis points, then choose **Special → Nonbreaking Space**. Alternatively, insert **^s** before the ellipsis points. (The caret mark (^) is above the number 6 on a QWERTY keyboard.)

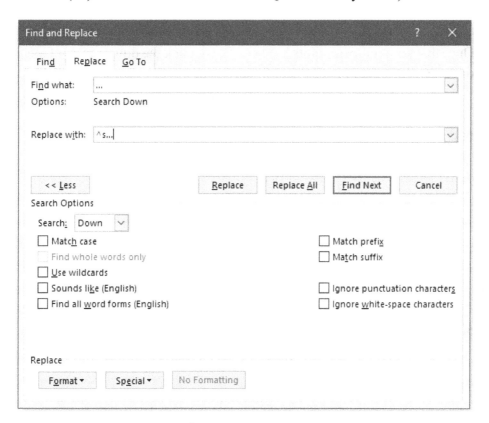

Figure 38: Formatting ellipsis points with a non-breaking space

Click **Find next** to be taken to the next set of ellipsis points then click **Replace** to replace them with a nonbreaking space attached. Repeat until all have been replaced.

Now the next thing to work out is if there are any sets of ellipsis points with single or multiple full-stops immediately following which weren't picked up during the first search. These are probably best fixed manually so rather than **Find and Replace**, simply paste a set of ellipsis points into the **Search document** field in your **Navigation pane**, without any space beforehand. Then place a single full-stop *immediately* after the ellipsis points, without leaving a space. Click **Results** and see if there are any ellipsis points which replaced four or more full-stops, leaving one or more full-stops behind. If so, click on that Result to be taken to that spot in the text and manually remove any errant full-stops, ensuring that there is a single space left after each set of ellipsis points.

Once that set of ellipsis points has been fixed, click the down arrow of the **Search document** box again to find and fix any others.

Notes:

A bit about dashes

A lot of people don't realise that there's a difference between:

- a hyphen -

- an en dash –

- and an em dash —

Each has is its own purpose and while there are myriad details to consider, there are some basic rules you can apply to keep your manuscript tidy and acceptable to the general population.

Hyphens

A hyphen is a small dash (use the minus sign - on the keyboard). It is used to join two words or syllables, or a syllable and a word, and takes no spacing either side. The idea of a hyphen is to help with ease of reading and for clarity, but they aren't always necessary.

For instance, *a delicately-flavoured tea* is perfectly acceptable and most readers will visually connect the first two words in their mind before reading 'tea'. However, the hyphen isn't all that necessary there as you can also write *a delicately flavoured tea* and the reader will still know what you're talking about.

But when you combine words which could be interpreted differently, a hyphen can help with clarity, especially in today's world where few people use commas in their writing! For instance, there's a difference between a *wide-angled lens* and a *wide angled lens*. If the second example truly related to a wide lens which had been placed at an angle, then there should be a comma after *wide*, but as commas are being used less and less in modern writing, one wouldn't really know for sure what the author meant!

Hyphens are used in numbers (*twenty-two*) and words where clarity is required to save the reader from having to re-read to interpret e.g. *de-ice* instead of *deice*, or *re-creation* (making again) instead of *recreation* (leisure activity).

Hyphens are often used to join multiple descriptors, such as in *up-to-date*. If in doubt about whether you need a hyphen or not between two words, consult an *up-to-date dictionary*. But it can also depend on your phrasing:

His knowledge was *up to date*.

This takes no hyphens because the two concepts – his knowledge and our assessment of it – have been separated. But consider:

He had *up-to-date* knowledge.

Here hyphens make it easier to read – we can quickly see as we're moving along that there's a group of words which describe what's coming, so we know to read those as one joined thing (the hyphens tell us that) and then apply that overall message to the next word.

There are many, many ways to use hyphens and this isn't a grammar book. The idea is to explain briefly the difference between the three types of dashes, so I'll move it along ...

En dashes

An en dash is about the size of a capital N, or two hyphens joined together, and is usually used as a linking device, but to link things that you wouldn't normally use a hyphen to link, such as date ranges (e.g. 1962–73). However, in running text in UK and Australian documents, it is often used with a space either side – like that, to indicate separation of thoughts, concepts, etc. US texts tend to take an unspaced em dash—like that—for separation of thoughts, concepts etc. (See below for more on the em dash.)

The easiest way to make an en dash is to type a spaced hyphen and let Word convert it. So type away, leave a space, press the minus/hyphen button, then the space bar again, then start typing the next word. If Word's settings are at default, then it will convert your spaced hyphen into an unspaced en dash – like that. If you can't get Word to create one automatically (if you're editing and text follows where you're typing, it won't always work), then you have two other options:

- Hold down **Ctrl** and press the **minus** key on the numerical keyboard of your PC. (Don't press the minus button above the letter P or you'll get this ugly thing:)

or

- Choose **Insert → Symbol → More Symbols → Special Characters** and then choose the en dash option from the list. That list also provides another keyboard shortcut for your en dash!

Once you've finished writing and editing your document, it's a good idea to search for spaced en dashes and insert a non-breaking space prior to each one to ensure that you don't end up with a new line starting with an en dash – like this one. The en dash here should be attached to the word 'dash' at the end of the line above so that the line looks like this:

to ensure that you don't end up with a new line starting with an en dash – like this one.

See the difference?

To insert a non-breaking space before your en dashes, highlight an en dash with your cursor, being careful not to pick up any spaces either side, then **right-click** and choose **Copy**.

Open your **Find and Replace** box and click in the **Find** field. **Right-click** and choose **Paste** to place the en dash in the Find field. Then click in the **Replace** field and **Paste** the en dash into that as well.

In the **Find** field, click in front of your en dash and place a single space, using your Space bar.

In the **Replace** field, click in front of your en dash and type ^s which is code for non-breaking space. The carat symbol is achieved by using **Shift** and pressing the number **6** on your typewriter keyboard, not your numeric keyboard (if you have one).

Click **Find Next** and when taken to that en dash, click **Replace** to replace the space with a non-breaking one. Continue until you've fixed all the en dashes in the document.

Notes:

_____

_____

_____

_____

_____

_____

_____

_____

_____

Em dashes

Em dashes, which are the approximate width equivalent of a capital M, are used more frequently in US publishing where Aussies and Brits would normally use a spaced en dash, but also have their use in British and Australian to indicate an abrupt change in the narrative, or to place emphasis on an explanation or insertion, or, in a way, in sense of brackets (parentheses).

However, their main use in British and Australian general writing and fiction is to indicate an interruption to someone's speech. In Australia, the rule is that the dash is used unspaced if it's indicating that part of a word is missing, and with a space if it's replacing an entire word and any text thereafter:

'I don't know if I —' (add a space beforehand as 'I' is a complete word)

'Yes, you can!' she yelled over her.

'Why don't you j—' (use unspaced as it replaces part of a word)

'Forget it!'

There is a variety in standards – some use the two-em dash to indicate a break in speech:

'I don't know if I ——'

'Yes, you can!' she yelled over her.

'Why don't you j——'

'Forget it!'

To insert an em dash, press **Alt** + **Ctrl** + **Minus** (on your Numerical keyboard if you have one), or else on your menu choose **Insert → Symbol → More Symbols** and **Special Characters** and choose it from the list there.

A word about dash choices

Different cultures use dashes differently. If you're writing fiction, or general non-fiction (as in, not academic or for government), then my suggestion is to choose a dash system which works for you and apply it consistently. You may still need two or three types of dashes in your document, for instance for a range of numbers you'll need an unspaced en dash (1842–1903) but to indicate an interruption to speech at the end of a sentence, you may prefer to use an em dash ('No! Please don't g—').

If you're writing non-fiction, then investigate the style manuals of universities in the area or country you're aiming your text at. They will give you an idea of 'the norm' for the sort of audience you're probably writing for.

Notes:

_____

_____

_____

_____

_____

_____

_____

_____

Standardise your dashes

Once you've made your dash decisions, it's a good idea to scroll through your document and look for ways your dashes have been used incorrectly or inconsistently. When you find such an instance, you can use Find and Replace to help you find other, similar instances, and fix them.

Have a look at the Table of Contents (ToC) that you created for *Roast Beef for Print*. Now that you've read the preceding paragraphs about dashes, is there anything odd you notice? Are some of the dashes different sizes? Do you have hyphens for Parts 2 and 3? This can happen in any document, so let's pretend this is a full-length novel and that we need to search the entire document for spaced hyphens where we should have a spaced en dash.

Click on the drop arrow in the **Search document** field at the top of your **Navigation** pane and choose **Replace,** (or, on your Home ribbon, click **Replace** at the far right) to bring up the **Find and Replace** dialogue box.

We're going to search for spaced hyphens (-) and replace them with a non-breaking space and an en dash (–). In the **Find** field, use your space bar to type a **space** then follow that with a **hyphen**.

In the **Replace** field, type **^s** for non-breaking space and ^= for en dash. Alternatively, click **More >>** then the drop arrow next to **Special** at the bottom of the dialogue box. From the Special menu, choose Non-breaking space. Repeat and choose **En dash**.

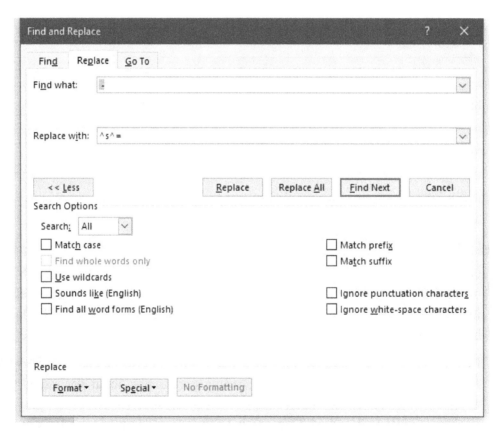

Figure 39: Setting up Find and Replace to change spaced hyphens to en dashes with a non-breaking space beforehand

Feel free to click the **<<Less** tab (centre, left) to hide the additional formatting dialogue so that you can see more of your document, then click **Find Next** to find the first spaced hyphen in your document. Assuming that it's a spaced hyphen which you wish to change to an en dash with a non-breaking space, then click **Replace**. Once replaced, Word should take you to the next spaced hyphen. Continue replacing spaced hyphens with en dashes until Word tells you that there are no more instances.

When using Find and Replace in a really large document, you can often click Replace All to do the job more quickly, but it's always good to manually replace a few instances of whatever you're changing first, in case there's a specific usage for whatever you're searching that you hadn't thought of. For instance, in a document where you've used a fancy spacer in Wingdings 2

you'd need to search for:

f e

to replace it with something else, as 'eff-space-ee' are the keystrokes behind the Wingdings 2 divider as shown.

However, if you were to replace the 'eff-space-ee' divider to, say:

* * *

and didn't do it one-by-one (you chose Replace All, rather than Find Next), you would end up changing phrases such as:

they jumped off each pier

to

they jumped of* * *ach pier

and you might not even notice!!

So jump carefully, Grasshopper.

Notes:

7. Now let's add some spice!

Learning aims of this chapter:

- Using fields to tailor your page headers and footers
- The cheat's way to tailor your ToC

Dynamic Page Headers

If you're writing a non-fiction book (like this one) you might like the chapter heading to appear at the top of each page, rather than the name of the book. There's a nifty way you can do this so that it happens automatically. Double-click in any of the headers which say *Roast Beef* (not *Paris Portingale*) to open the Header and Footer ribbon. In the ribbon, towards the left hand end, you'll find an item called **Quick Parts**. Click on the drop arrow and choose **Field**.

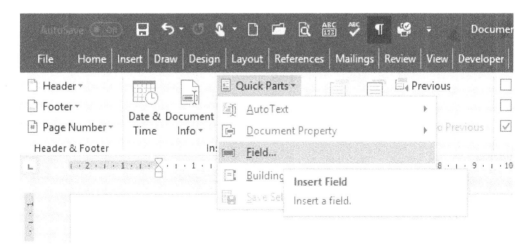

Figure 40 : Locating the Field insertion menu

In the **Field** dialogue box choose, ensure that **(All)** is showing for **Categories**, then choose **StyleRef** from the **Field name** list, click on **Heading 1** in the centre panel, check **Preserve formatting during updates**, then click **OK**.

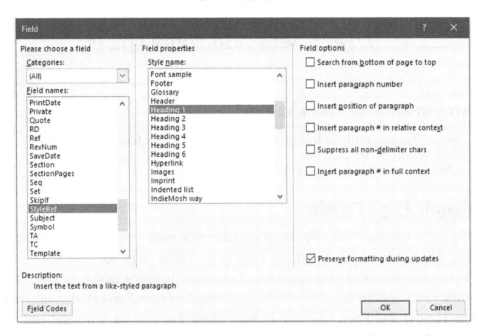

Figure 41 : Setting the Style Ref options for your header (or footer)

Double-click on the body of your document to exit the Header and Footer ribbon, and go to **Print Preview**. As you scroll through the document, you should see the headers on the right hand pages change to *Part 1 – Graham*, *Part 2 – Johanna*, etc.

Notes:

_____

_____

_____

_____

_____

Different ToC entries to the page headings

Sometimes our authors want to see the word 'chapter', or 'part', or 'book' on the page where the section starts, but don't want the word repeated in the ToC.

In *Roast Beef*, each chapter is headed along the convention of:

Part X – Name

Let's say Paris has decided that he wants the ToC listing to show:

X: Name

rather than using the word 'Part' and a dash between the number and name. However, he wants to keep 'Part X – Name' as the heading on the first page of each chapter. Tricky, huh?

The easiest way to do this is to create an additional, hidden heading on the actual chapter page for Word to draw through for the ToC.

Create 'dummy' headings

To do this, go to the first page of the chapter **Part 1 – Graham**, and highlight that entire heading line. **Copy** (either right-click copy or Ctrl-C), and then place your cursor at the beginning of the line and **Paste** the heading in again (either **right-click Paste** or **Ctrl-V**). The top of your page will now have *Part 1 – Graham* showing as two headings.

What we're going to do is make the first heading the one which draws through to the ToC – so we'll leave that as Heading 1. We'll make the second one the page and chapter heading, and so we'll make that Heading 2.

(Just bear in mind that if you're using fields to create the page headers, you may need to adjust your page header field to point at Heading 2, otherwise you'll have the new Heading 1 text in your header. That may be what you want, so in that case, don't do anything!)

Create new Heading 2 to match Heading 1 style

Click anywhere in the line of the second heading. **Point** at **Heading 2** on your **Styles pane**, click the **drop arrow** and choose **Update Heading 2 to Match Selection**. This will make both heading styles identical.

Create hidden Heading 1 style for ToC

Now click on the first heading and bring up the **Modify Styles** dialogue box for **Heading 1**. Change the **font size** to the smallest size possible – usually an **8 pt** – and change the font to **Times New Roman** as that's a reasonably small font to start with. Click **Format → Paragraph** and make sure that spacing is **0 pt Before**, **0 pt After** and **Single line spacing**. Click **OK**, then **OK** again.

The top of your page should now look something like this:

Part 1 – Graham

Part 1 – Graham

However, if the top of your page looks like this:

Part 1 – Graham

Part 1 – Graham

then you'll need to Modify Heading 2, as it's probably based on Heading 1. And changing Heading 1 has also changed Heading 2.

Before you do anything, click **Ctrl-Z** to undo the change to Heading Style 1. This should change both headings back to:

Part 1 – Graham

Part 1 – Graham

Point at the second heading and bring up the **Modify style** dialogue box. Make a note of the style choices – font, font size, alignment, paragraph and line spacing etc. **Close** the Modify style box.

Now click Ctrl-Y to reverse the Ctrl-Z you pressed above – this should revert the headings back to:

Part 1 – Graham

Part 1 – Graham

If you click anywhere in the first line, your Styles pane should show that it's Heading 1. If you click in the second line, it should show that it's Heading 2.

Bring up the dialogue box to **Modify** Heading 2 (by clicking on the drop arrow). **Click** the **drop arrow** next to **Style Based on** to change it from Heading 1 to

Normal. You'll now need to reinstate the font, size, alignment etc of your original Heading 1 choices, as per the note you made. Click OK and OK and your headings should now look something like this:

Part 1 – Graham

Part 1 – Graham

Save your document and head to Part 2 –Johanna.

You'll notice that the headings for all the other sections are now smaller – in line with the new format for Heading 1. So the first page for Part 2 –Johanna will look like this:

Part 2 – Johanna

That's okay. **Copy** and **paste** the heading in front of itself so that you have two headings for Part 2:

Part 2 – Johanna

Part 2 – Johanna

Now place your cursor anywhere in the *second* heading, without highlighting any particular word or letter, and click on **Heading 2** in your **Styles** pane so that you now have:

Part 2 – Johanna

Part 2 – Johanna

Rinse and repeat for Parts 3, 4 and 5.

Update the heading text in the document

We're now going to replace the word **Part** at the beginning of each Heading 1 line with the *number* of that part, followed by a colon. So instead of:

Part 2 – Johanna

we'll be making it:

2: Johanna

And we're going to pretend that this is a big document and so we need to use Find and Replace.

Open **Find and Replace** and in the **Find** field type **Part** (with a capital P) and a **single space** after it. Click **More** → **Match case**.

Ensure that the **Replace** field is empty. Click **Find Next** and then **Replace** to delete the first instance of Part and the single space following.

When that's done, the cursor will move to the next heading, below. But we don't want to change *that* heading, so click **Find Next**. We're only deleting 'Part' and the ensuing space from Heading 1, *not* Heading 2.

Once you've finished, each chapter heading should look like this:

1 – Graham

Part 1 – Graham

The next step is to delete the space and the en dash after the number and replace them with a colon to change 1– Graham to 1: Graham.

In your **Find** field, type a **space** immediately followed by ^= as the shortcut for an en dash. In the **Replace** field type a colon **:** noting that a colon is the one with two dots, achieved by using the Shift key (as opposed to a semi-colon, which is the dot above a comma, achieved by pressing the same key, but without Shift). Ensure that **Match case** has been *un*checked.

Click **Find next** and replace each of the five Heading 1 instances of a spaced en dash with a colon, being careful not to replace any en dashes in the body of the document, or any of the Heading 2 en dashes. When you've finished, each chapter heading should look like this:

1: Graham

Part 1 – Graham

Using wild cards to find and replace

Word does have the capacity for you to use wild cards (symbols meant to designate a range of characters) so that you could possibly replace each **Part X –** with **Part X:** in one Find and Replace action, but that's getting into the sort of advanced territory that's beyond the scope of this book. However, if you're interested in playing with wildcards, search 'find and replace with wild cards in word' and you'll find a mountain of videos and blog posts to help you.

Update the ToC with the new headings

Now go back to your ToC, right-click and choose **Update field → Update entire table**. You may not have to click Update entire table – sometimes Word is a step ahead and knows that that job has to be done!

Your ToC should now be listing the parts like this:

> 1: Graham

> 2: Johanna

> 3: Graham

> 4: Johanna

> 5: The Car Park

and so on. However, if you find your ToC is showing:

> 1: Graham

> Part 1 – Graham

> 2: Johanna

> Part 2 – Johanna

> 3: Graham

> Part 3 – Graham

and so on, then that will be because it's picking up the new Heading 2 items.

If that's the case, point at the ToC, right-click and choose **Edit Field**. In the dialogue box, under **Categories**: select **Index and Tables**, then highlight **TOC** in the section below that.

Ensure that there's a tick in the box in the lower right-hand side of the dialogue box to **Preserve formatting during updates** then click **Table of Contents** towards the centre top of the dialogue box.

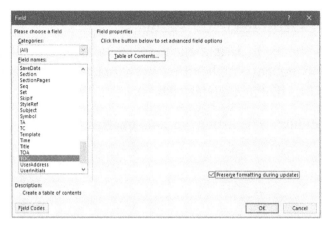

Figure 42 : Wrangling your Table of Contents

When the Table of Contents dialogue box opens, towards the bottom is an option to show a set number of Heading levels. Change this from **3** to **1**, so that the ToC only picks up Heading 1 entries. Click **OK** and return to the ToC, accepting the option to update. Your ToC should now list numbers and names only.

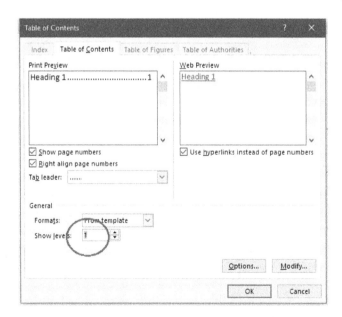

Figure 43 : Limiting your ToC to Heading 1 entries only

Cleaning up the excess headers in the body of the text

Obviously, we don't want two headings on each page, so point at any of the headings in the ToC, and **Ctrl-left click** to be taken to that page. Click on the first heading – the little Heading 1 at the top of the page. On your **Styles** pane, choose to **Modify Heading 1**. When the dialogue box opens, change the **font colour** for Heading 1 to **White**, rather than Automatic. Click **OK** and return to your document. As you scroll through, you'll notice that the little headings at the top have 'disappeared'. They haven't really – they're still there – but they won't print and your ToC will show only the part number and person's name from now on.

Warning 1

If you do any work on the headings – change them in any way – you'll have to remember to change *both* headings, the visible Heading 2 and the invisible Heading 1, otherwise your ToC won't match your pages. For instance, let's say Paris decides to change *Graham* to *Graeme* – you're going to have to remember to change *all* instances, otherwise your ToC won't show the right name!

However, it's as easy as modifying Heading 1 to show in any colour you choose while you're working on the alterations before turning it back to white when you've finished.

Warning 2

If you decided to use Field formatting to draw the chapter name through to the page header, then you'll need to consider whether that needs updating or not. The question will be: What do you (or Paris) want showing in the header? Part X – Name or X: Name?

If it's the latter (the new Heading 1 style), then no worries – the headers will update automatically. But if you want the full heading showing – the new Heading 2 – you will need to double-click on one of the chapter headers, click on the drop arrow next to **Quick Parts** and choose **Field**.

In the **Field** dialogue box choose, ensure that **(All)** is showing for **Categories**, then choose **StyleRef** from the **Field name** list, click on **Heading 2** in the centre panel, check **Preserve formatting during updates**, then click **OK**.

Double-click on the body of your document to exit the Header and Footer ribbon, and go to **Print Preview**. As you scroll through the document, you should see the headers on the right hand pages have changed to 1: Graham, 2: Johanna, etc.

Notes:

8. Time to serve up

Learning aims of this chapter:

- Things to review before hitting the 'Print' button

Is it cooked?

Once you've reached the point where you feel you've got everything sitting where you want, it's time to check to make sure that you really have wrangled everything to taste. Here's a list of things to look for:

Any blank pages?

First up, zoom out so that you can see at least three or four pages to a row, and check for any inadvertent blank pages. These will be ones where there's one empty line too many, and the page break has slipped over to the next page. On your menu, click **View → Multiple Pages**. Then press **Ctrl** and **scroll** back towards yourself with your mouse, to zoom out further Alternatively, drag the zoom bar at the bottom right hand side of your screen.

Scroll through the document and zoom in to remove any errant empty line breaks creating an unnecessarily blank page. Zoom out and scroll to the next one. When finished, **update your ToC** to reflect any changes.

Any pages with just a line or two on them?

It's amazing how you can work on a book for ages, and then suddenly, just when you're ready to export, you notice a page at the end of a chapter with one or two lousy little lines at the top. They can arise from the smallest of tweaks elsewhere, so scroll through and make sure you don't have any, or if you do, that you're happy to keep them. If you want them gone, then you'll need to edit some text in that chapter, or change some character spacing or paragraph breaks See Chapter 6 on fixing widows and orphans for ideas.

Are page numbers correct?

Page numbers should generally start with 1 for the first page of the main text, and be in Roman numerals (i, ii, iv, xiii etc) in the introductory pages. And if you have separate sections throughout the book, does each section continue on from the numbering before, or do you have the odd section which starts from 1 again?!

Are headers and footers suppressed where expected?

If you've introduced internal title pages to your books and these are meant not to have any page numbering or headers, then are they showing as expected?

The quickest and cleanest way to check these is to click on **Headings** in your **Navigation pane**, and then click on each title page to go straight to it. If any of these pages have unexpected headers or footers, you'll need to click in the header or footer and see what the issue is.

The problem will usually be that it's linked to the previous header or footer. If that's the case, then click **Link to Previous** so that it's not highlighted. Then check the following pages and sections to make sure that their headers and footers are still correct!

Are blank pages and new sections sitting where expected?

When you add section breaks such as an Odd Page section break, Word won't show any blank pages in the typing screen. However, it will show them in the Print Preview screen, so click on your Print Preview icon if you have it on your Quick Access toolbar, or else choose **File → Print** to see a print preview of your book. Scroll through and check that the pages you expect to see on the left and right are where they should be.

Has my ToC updated correctly?

Always, *always* check your ToC before exporting your files for print. Quite often, especially in complex books, the ToC will often update and show everything as being on page 2, or some other page! This is only temporary – it just needs you to go to the ToC and updated it. However, it will often revert back to the repetitive page numbering depending on what changes you've made to the file, so always double check that your ToC is up to date prior to exporting any files.

Do my 'guff' pages look correct?

In **Print Preview** mode, check that your half-title and/or title page, your imprint/copyright page, dedication and other introductory pages look correct. Have headers and page numbers been suppressed from the title, imprint, dedication, 'also by', reviews pages? Are any page numbers showing here in Roman numerals (i, ii, iii) and not Arabic (1, 2, 3)? Is vertical justification on or off, and is text sitting where you'd expect on the page?

Do my end pages look correct?

Scroll through to the end of your book and check that the last page looks correct, that the next page which follows is what you'd expect, and that numbering, headers, footers etc, are what you'd expect on these last pages. For instance, of you have an 'About the Author' page, does it have a page header? If so, does it say 'About the Author' or is it drawing from the last chapter of the book, if you used fields to create your page headers with?

Notes:

_____

_____

_____

_____

_____

_____

_____

_____

Export to PDF

Once you think your Word doc is looking good, it's time to export it to PDF.

If you use Adobe Acrobat DC, then you can use **File → Save as Adobe PDF**.

If not, then you should be able to use **File → Save as** and then choose **PDF** from the file format drop arrow below the **File Name** field.

Note to Adobe users: If you find that a font doesn't embed properly when you choose 'Save as Adobe PDF', then try using Word's native PDF compiler instead.

Give your file a meaningful name, such as *Roast Beef for Print V1*. (The use of 'V' means 'version'.) If you make changes to your Word doc, then it's useful to save subsequent PDFs as V1.1, V1.2 for minor changes, and V2, V3 for major changes. If you write over your prior PDF with a new one, and then realise you've made a change that's introduced an error, you've lost the prior PDF and don't have a stepping-stone to compare to.

Once you've reached a PDF point where you're happy with the files you have, then you can consider deleting or archiving earlier versions.

Check your PDF

Open your PDF in your PDF viewer. Most viewers will allow you to view the file in book layout if you choose the right viewing options.

In Adobe Acrobat, you can get it to lay out like a book, with two pages side by side, by clicking on your menu:

1. **View → Page Display → Two Page View** to get it to show two pages at a time, then

2. **View → Page Display → Show Cover Page in Two Page View** to get the odd numbered pages on the right and the even numbered pages on the left. The cover page will sit by itself on the right.

Scroll through, checking to make sure that everything is as expected. If not, make a list of any issues and where they are. When finished, go back to your Word doc, make your changes, update the ToC, then export a fresh PDF with an updated version number at the end of the file name.

Check your PDF's properties

With your PDF open, click **File → Properties → Description** (if using Adobe Acrobat) to check that your PDF page size is correct. This is most important!

Then click the **Fonts** tab to make sure that all fonts have been embedded.

Notes:

_____

_____

_____

_____

_____

_____

Exporting a PDF for print

Unfortunately, every printing company, no matter how small or large, will have different specs for the type of PDF they require, so you'll need to do your research and find out what they need, if you can do it, if they can do it for you, or if you have to pay someone else to do it for you.

However, Smashwords, Amazon's CreateSpace and Amazon's KDP platforms will all allow you to upload a Word doc for your internals file. Results may not be quite what you expect, however, so please bear that in mind.

9. Looking back

Why did we have to nuke the original copy of *Roast Beef*?

If you cast your mind back to the beginning of this exercise, you'll recall that you started by 'nuking' the copy of *Roast Beef* which you'd downloaded from my website. Now that you've been working with Word's Styles function and have a handle on how useful it is, it might be interesting for you to see what I see when I open someone else's document. So I want you to open the file you downloaded – the original *Roast Beef* file.

Once it's open onscreen, click on the expansion arrow at the bottom right hand side of the **Styles** option in the ribbon menu to open up the **Styles pane**. Dock the pane to the side of your screen if Word hasn't automatically done that. Now go to the bottom of the Styles pane and click **Options...** to open the Options dialogue box. Here's a reminder of what we're looking for:

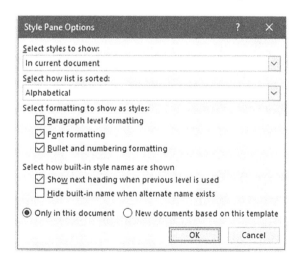

Figure 44 : Calling up the styles in this document

In the Options dialogue box, please choose **In current document** from the first drop-down, and **Alphabetical** from the next drop-down. Then tick the first four of the five option boxes and then **Only in this document** before finishing with **OK**.

Now look at the **Styles pane**. Scroll up and down and take note of the various formatting options which have been applied to different parts of the file. There aren't many there, but you can see that they're ad-hoc, applied randomly and without planning. (Please note that most of these have been applied by me for the purposes of this exercise. Paris delivers very neat and clean manuscripts!)

If you wanted to change the formatting, you'd have to highlight paragraph by paragraph, skipping the headings, and perhaps skipping the first paragraph in each section if you wanted those to have different indents.

However, in *Roast Beef for Print*, if you wanted to change the indents used for the body of the text, all you'd have to do is Modify the Story style and it would be done, right throughout the book.

Using Word's Styles allows you to do so much with so few keystrokes.

Locating errant formats

Sometimes, even when you're formatting a 'clean' or 'nuked' document, an errant style will creep in without you realising. All of a sudden, you'll be looking at your Styles pane and think, 'Well, where the [insert favourite swear word] did THAT style come from?!'

To locate an errant style in the original *Roast Beef* file, open the Styles pane and, ensuring that it shows only styles in the current document (start by clicking **Options** at the foot of the Styles pane), and have a look at the styles in the original file.

What styles can you see? Can you see one called +**Body (Calibri), 11 pt**? If so, **point** at it, click the drop-down arrow and choose **Select All 1 Instances**. This will take you to the paragraph in question. Look at it. Can you see how it differs ever so slightly from the paragraphs before and after?

If you can't see it, then turn your paragraph marks on. How is it different? Would you have picked that up just by scrolling through the manuscript? You might now that you've completed these formatting exercises, but I bet you wouldn't have without them.

To rectify it, ensure that your cursor is on that line (without highlighting any word in particular), then click on the style simply called **Arial** to apply that style to that line, and watch as **+Body (Calibri), 11 pt** disappears from the Styles pane.

Investigate some of the other styles in the Styles pane, such as First line: 0.5 cm and see where they are, and the effect they have on the text.

Feel free to close the original *Roast Beef* file without saving any of your changes, then you can go through this exercise again as a refresher should you need it at any stage.

Notes:

10. Quick reference

This book is intended to help get you started, to give you enough to work with to help address the most common things today's novelist is likely to want to do with their text. But it's just an entrée from the banquet menu.

If you're after choices from the à la carte, then the internet, if you haven't worked it out by now, is a veritable treasure trove of detail delivered in blog posts and videos, assuming you know what you're looking for. But after a bit of search practice, you'll find answers to most of your questions there.

In the meantime, though, here's a mini database of *some* of the terms, handy hints and shortcuts that we use frequently at MoshPit Publishing:

Tools to become *real* friendly with

Ctrl-Z or the **Undo** button – your best friend(s)!

Paragraph marks – add them to your **Quick Access Toolbar** to easily turn off and on.

Print Preview – add to your **Quick Access Toolbar** to get a cleaner view of your document quickly.

Navigation Pane – for quickly locating things in a large document and for having a handy overview of the document by your side.

Styles Pane – when sorted alphabetically will help you see better what styles you've used where.

Status Bar – will give you a quick overall view of your page and word count, the section you're working in, the line you're on – adapt to suit your needs.

Terms

Quick Access Toolbar – the row of little icons at the very top of Word for the tools you use the most.

The ribbon – this is the main menu in MS Office, and shows tabs for File, Home, Insert, Draw, design, Layout, Reference and so on.

Context menu/Pop up menu – this is a mini-menu which opens up depending on how you're using Word (or any MS Office product) and where your cursor is placed at that moment. The most common context menu appears after right-clicking with your mouse.

Drop arrow – the arrow to the side of a menu option which allows you to access more refined menu options.

Headers and footers – these are the repeated lines at the top and/or bottom of each page which will contain quick reference information such as and or all of the following: the page number, the title of the book, the name of the author, the chapter you're reading.

Headings – these are the navigation tools your reader will use to know where they are in the book and what the following text will be talking about. Try not to use more than four or five levels of heading, unless absolutely necessary.

Tailoring

Quick Access Toolbar

On your ribbon, click **File → Options → Quick Access Toolbar**. Change the first drop arrow to **All Commands** if you can't find what you're looking for in the **Popular Commands**. When you find a tool you want on the left, click on it then click **Add** between the two lists. You should now see it in the right hand column – **Customize Quick Access Toolbar**. Then use the arrows to the right of that to move the items up and down into your preferred order. (Up moves items to the left while down moves them to the right on the toolbar.) Click **OK** when done to save.

Navigation pane

On your ribbon, click the drop arrow next to **Find** at the far right hand side of your screen. Click **Find** to open the **Navigation pane**. Drag it to the left or right of your document to 'dock' it in place on your screen.

Styles pane

Click on the drop arrow at the bottom right hand side of the **Styles** box in your ribbon menu to pop out the **Styles pane**. Drag it to the left or right of your document to 'dock' it in place on your screen.

We generally have our Navigation pane to the far left of our screen, then the Styles pane, then the document.

Show two pages or more at a time

Click on **View** on your ribbon, then choose **Multiple Pages** to show more than one page at a time on your screen. Use Ctrl and scroll forwards and backwards with your mouse to zoom in and out and increase and decrease the number of pages you wish to see at any one time.

Tricks of the trade

- Double-click to highlight a word.

- Triple-click to highlight a whole paragraph.

- Double-click in a header or footer for the Header/Footer menus.

- Ctrl-A will highlight everything.

- Ctrl-B will make **bold** everything you've highlighted.

- Ctrl-C will copy whatever you've highlighted.

- Ctrl-F will open the search or 'Find' box. (This even works when you're on the internet, which is very handy for searching for particular terms on a web page!)

- Ctrl-I will *italicise* everything you've highlighted.

- Ctrl-S will save your document with the same file name.

- Ctrl-U will underline everything you've highlighted. Underlining or underscoring isn't recommended in print these days as it's hard to read and can also suggest a URL. Underlining harks back to the days of typewriters when we didn't have italics or bold to emphasise text.

- Ctrl-V will paste the last thing you copied or cut into your document exactly where your cursor is. Watch for the context menu to allow you to paste with or without formatting.

- Ctrl-X will cut whatever you've highlighted.

- Ctrl-Y – will redo your last action. This is very handy if you've just formatted a word or phrase a certain way and don't wish to repeat the mouse-clicking for the next half a dozen you have to format. Just highlight the next word or phrase and press Ctrl-Y and it should apply the formatting for you! Rinse and repeat.

- Ctrl-Z will undo the last thing you did. Keep pressing to step backwards.

- Ctrl-Enter will insert a page break.

- Shift-Enter will insert a 'soft' line break.

- Ctrl-Shift-Space will insert a non-breaking space.

- Ctrl-Minus will enter an en dash: –

- Ctrl-Alt-Minus will enter an em dash: —

- Minus-Minus-> will create an in-text arrow: →

- Ctrl-Scroll forward (on your mouse) will zoom in on your document/screen.

- Ctrl-Scroll back (on your mouse) will zoom out on your document/screen.

- Ctrl-Alt-Full-stop will insert a set of ellipsis points

- Ctrl-Alt-Space will turn on Text-to-Speech and read your document out loud to you!

11. The wash-up

Preparing your book for print is both exciting and scary. The process will often draw your attention to things you might have done better, or things you hadn't considered previously. While that can be annoying or unsettling, now's the time to find out – while you can still fix things!

This book doesn't have all the answers, but it should help get you on your way to preparing a reasonably neat manuscript and introducing you to a range of tools you can use to wrangle your document so that you can produce something that looks like a book and not a manuscript. With practice and exploration, you might even make a career out of being a book formatter. Or not, if this book helps you realise that formatting is just not for you and that it's worth paying someone else to do it! And if that's the case, then it was worth the investment to save you the headaches.

Getting your manuscript ready is still just one part of the publishing process. You will need to assign ISBNs and organise a cover file and then actually publish the book somewhere, somehow. Hopefully you've already planned most of that before getting to this stage.

I find that it helps to write my books in the page layout that I expect to print them in. This book started as a 6 x 9 but, after a lot of consideration, I changed it to the 7.5 x 9.25 inch paperback you're holding.

So horses for courses, whatever works for you. And that's the beauty of self publishing!

12. Acknowledgements

This book has been a long time in the cooking, so first up I have to thank my incredibly patient husband, Wayne, for putting up with at least two years' worth of 'I must finish my formatting book this month'. If you're reading this, then I finally made it!

Next cab off the rank is the also incredibly patient Paris Portingale who gave permission around three years ago for me to use the delightful *Roast Beef* as the sample text for this book. It was the perfect story to provide the variety of options I needed to demonstrate.

And those demonstrations were ably tested by my wonderful team of 'crash-test dummies':

- Alix Kwan of moxieediting.com.au
- Debbie Watson of getitrightproofreading.com.au
- Sally-Anne Watson Kane of ontimetyping.com

Thank you all for your patience, expertise and great feedback.

Thanks to Ally Mosher, my daughter, offsider and 'trusty sidekick' who's worked alongside me for nearly nine years now, helping me develop IndieMosh, our self publishing facilitation service for Australian authors, and One Thousand Words Plus, our book promotion site, not to mention a bunch of other projects plus more than three hundred titles for our clients. Without Ally and her technical expertise, I wouldn't have achieved half of what I've achieved in the last ten years.

Thanks of a different kind must go to my first-born, Sara, who sets a great self-development example which encourages me to keep challenging myself. I'd be a much less-aware person in a totally different place without her in my life.

Next, I need to acknowledge the incredibly selfless people who take the time to blog and record videos which they then post to the internet to help others with their tasks, whatever they may be. Although I've learnt a lot from attending workshops, collaborating with others, buying books over the last ten years, and making my own mistakes, I've also benefitted greatly from the generosity of others who have taken the time to share their knowledge so freely. There is no one individual site or book or person I have depended on – I find I search for what I need and go where the path seems most promising, and this book has been written from those accumulated and combined learnings over the years and not from any one source. Many of my learnings have also been adapted to my needs, so again, it's what works best for me. However, if you are looking for sources on the internet, some of the best I can refer you to are:

- The Smashwords Style Guide: https://www.smashwords.com/books/view/52

- Microsoft Office Help for Word: https://support.office.com/en-us/word or https://support.office.com/en-au/word – will probably divert to the correct page automatically depending on how your computer is set up

- Suzanne S Barnhill's Word FAQs at http://wordfaqs.ssbarnhill.com/

- Word Ribbon Tips at https://wordribbon.tips.net/index.html, particularly those by Allen Wyatt

Finally, I'd like to thank you, the reader, for coming along on this journey with me. I hope that you've achieved something from this book, whether that be a better understanding of things you can do to make your documents – not just a book, but any document – look neater more easily, or whether it all seems too much and you're happy to acknowledge your limitations and leave this fussiness to someone else. So long as it's helped you work out a way forward that suits you, then that's enough for me.

I wish you all the best for your journey, wherever you're headed.

Jenny Mosher

13. About the Author

I'm an accountant by trade who fell into helping people self publish after a mid-life career change via editing. The one thing I've learned in life is that nothing you learn is ever wasted.

When I'm not helping Australian authors self publish via **IndieMosh.com.au** I'm trying to write my next book. I seem to be drawn towards non-fiction around self publishing lately, but one day I hope to get out of that and into some fun pulp fiction. One day!

In the meantime, I relax by bushwalking, painting, hunting dead relatives for my ever-expanding family trees, making papier mâché bowls from recycled paper and spending time with family and friends.

To find out more, visit my self-indulgent, occasionally updated, occasionally opinionated blog and website at **jennifermosher.com.au**

Thanks for your time, and happy writing!

Jenny Mosher

www.ingramcontent.com/pod-product-compliance
Lightning Source LLC
Chambersburg PA
CBHW060144060326
40690CB00018B/3971